The Falls of Green Mountain

The Story of a Butterfly

A Novella by

James Kaye

www.trafford.com
North America & international
toll-free: 1 888 232 4444 (USA & Canada)
fax: 812 355 4082

Plate 1.
Parnassius smintheus Doubleday 1874
Rocky Mountain Apollo Plate XXXIX
W.J. Holland 1898 The Butterfly Book
Variations in Wing Patterns

Dedication

To those who ever chased butterflies and when fast on the run over and across obstacles such as fences, creeks, rocks, logs, and through gardens and farm fields and over and through meadows and marshes and along the edges of woods where poison ivy, thorny bushes, cactuses and thistles grew.

American Painted Lady on a Thistle
Gouche on paper © Katie Lee

Front Cover. Waterfalls. USNPS Public Domain image.
© Fig. 8. Image in *Colorado Midland* by Morris Cafky.
© Fig. 9. Image from Revelstoke Railroad Museum.

The Falls of Green Mountain
The Story of a Butterfly

Green Mountain Falls, Colorado, May, 1889

"Do you remember when we first met?"
(Kenneth Stanley, Protagonist **Fig. 1**)
"Yes. It was the day you first saw me and said 'hello.'"
(Sally Ruth, Heroine **Fig. 2**)
What follows is a story of friendship in a scenic valley
with picturesque waterfalls, a small town with a new railroad,
a hotel and a lake, and all amid the montane homes of
Rocky Mountain Apollo butterflies
aka Snow Butterflies of the Mountains.

A Novella
(A Long Short Story)
by

James Kaye

The Falls of Green Mountain

"Hello. Do you have a single vacancy for a week?" The tall young man with a British accent asked the lovely young lady at the registration desk in the Antlers Hotel in May of 1889,

(**Fig. 3**) and it so named for its large collection of deer and elk trophies. Kenneth Stanley looked about impressed by so many of them then back more impressed by the  receptionist girl's youthful beauty with chestnut-colored curly hair and big brown eyes.

"Yes" she replied with a smile, likewise returned. "We have a vacant room with a balcony looking out upon the snow-capped mountains of the Continental Divide. You'll have a good view of Pike's Peak which is up over 14,000 feet in height."

"Yes" the young man replied. "'I could see the peak from afar when coming here by rail." He then registered his name and home address. The receptionist read the information and handed him the key to a top floor room.

"I see you are from London Mr. Stanley. We have a lot of guests who visit here from England and some British families from London have moved here. This town is fast becoming nick-named 'Little London.'" She said with another big smile. "And in case you didn't know, Mr. Stanley, there is a troupe of London stage players now touring America and quite coincidental to your arrival they will be here Saturday morning to perform the Payne and Irving comedy, *King Charles the Second* for hotel guests, employees and a few of our city dignitaries."

> [During early colonial times, traveling actors and troupes from London took the first tentative steps in establishing America's theatrical tradition, and of the sixteen best plays of the period *King Charles the Second* was rated number three.]

"That *is* coincidental since just last year I saw *King Charles the Second* in the London Royal Opera House. It was the Drury Lane Troupe actors and it is a great comedy which drew standing ovations. You will like it."

"What's it about?"

"It's about King Charles the Second's fascination of a pretty girl named Mary. The King goes incognito to the tavern where she lives with her uncle, the owner, to see and meet her, and all the things that happen are funny. If Mary is the same singer in the Troupe performing here, you will like her. She has a beautiful soprano voice."

"I know from having helped make their reservations and plans for what to do while here that some want to hike to the top of Pike's Peak, and then another day to go up Ute Pass to the natural rock formations of the Garden of the Gods and inside the Cave of the Winds. In exchange for their gratis play to the hotel staff and guests, General Palmer, the owner, has offered them free accommodations and meals, and leaving to them the use of one of our hotel omnibuses with a driver to go where they want on sightseeing trips."

"I would like to hear the soprano again and will make plans, but one day I too want to hike up the peak but only as far as the snowline."

"Why stop there, Mr. Stanley, when you would be so close to the summit?"

"It's because there are no meadows above it." He grinned. "I want to walk around through some of those on the way up because in such open sunnier habitats is where endemic species of plants and animals are normally found but seldom elsewhere. It's unfortunate in England these days that so many of the country's once natural meadows have been plowed over for hay fields and pasture lands for grazing cattle to leave little to nothing of anything native."

"That's sad to hear, but why such interest in undisturbed meadows?"

"It's because I am a butterfly collector, and I work for the British Museum of Natural History for a Mr. Edward Doubleday who is the imminent entomologist and butterfly expert there. In 1847 now some forty years ago he described and named a species of one of the Parnassian butterflies as *Parnassius smintheus*, named after the Greek God Apollo Smintheus and found here in the Rocky Mountains. He is quite elderly now but is still interested in furthering his studies of the morphological differences among Parnassians, or Mountain Apollos as they are commonly called."

"I know nothing of anything of that sort." Sally admitted. "It's all Greek to me." She laughed.

In being eager to continue conversing with the very pretty and immediately likeable girl with such an engaging smile and a pleasing voice, Kenneth Stanley continued to explain that Parnassian butterflies are found in montane regions around the world. "England though," he added, "has no mountains high enough to have snow lines which when living that high is why Parnassian butterflies are sometimes known as Snow Apollos."

"How interesting, and what's the interest in their morphological features that you mentioned?"

"Well, it's that they can vary in body color based on how high they live, called altitudinal melanism. The darker bodies at high elevations help them warm up faster in the morning sun and why they mostly live out in sunny meadows and not in forests. Too, Mountain Apollos that live in the higher elevations tend to be a little smaller."

"Why is that?"

"It's because when living up to snow lines, the coldness that high slows down their metabolism and where there is less plant food for them. Moreover, to better identify closely related Apollos, there are the anatomical differences between their... their...." Ken stopped suddenly to not say anything more of the need to dissect and compare differences in the inner and outer parts of Apollo female genitalia, and after copulating, and with their special glands, males secrete a gelatinous so-called mating plug that seal females with a sort of chastity belt in order to avoid sperm competition with other males. Oops! He had to think. Such said would no doubt embarrass the young lady to hear of it.

> [Without telling Sally what might be embarrassing to her to hear was that females of both halves of the Class Insecta and Order Lepidoptera, the butterflies and moths, have some of the most complicated genitalia and peculiar sex habits in the insect world.]

"I, uh, was just going to say that there are some things about Apollo anatomy in need of further research, and the reason I will collect more to take back when I return to England."

"Oh! And thanks for the information Mr. Stanley. I never knew anything of such interest about butterflies, but they are pretty and I do like to see them."

"Me too! But please there is no need to call me 'Mr.' thank you. I go by my nickname 'Ken' but never by 'Kenny.'" He laughed. "And may I call you Sally? I notice the 'Sally Ruth' on your name badge."

"That's okay…Ken." She said, hesitatingly with a shy smile to say his first name as asked. "I'm Sally with a 'y' but never with an 'ie,' thank you," so said in delightful humor to mimic Ken. Both laughed.

"Well then, thank you for the honor, but what's your surname?"

"I'm just plain ole Sally Ruth, nothing more. Ruth is my birth family name though I don't know much about the origin of it. I was once told it might be German or Scandinavian."

"Could be, maybe, but where are you from…somewhere in Germany, perhaps?"

"Oh no," she laughed, "I was born in a little place called Park Ridge, in Illinois up northwest of Chicago a few miles and my sister, Sue, two years older than me, and I moved here three years ago and when I got this hotel job as a receptionist. We lived awhile on North Tejon Street close to here but then my sister died, and General Palmer gave me a room here in his hotel to live and to include all of my meals when I eat in the dining room. He is such a nice old gentleman. I love him like a father, and he looks after me like a daughter, bless him."

"I'm sorry to hear about your sister. How old was she when she died?"

"She was twenty-three."

"Why in the first place did the two of you come all this way to live?"

"Sue and I were looking for a bit more excitement in our lives, more than in dull old Park Ridge," Sally laughed, "and we had read some interesting and thrilling adventure stories of the so-called wild west and all...the cowboys and Indians kind of stuff you know...but as you can see, Colorado Springs is now a bustling city with twenty thousand people and not at all wild. There are, though, some renegade Indians still roaming around up in the mountains. The Governor had campaigned on a theme that the Utes must go and one time not long ago an Indian agent was killed by some not wanting to be captured and moved onto a reservation. Now and then the wilder of them still hiding out occasionally rustle cattle in need of food, and ranchers jokingly say their cows are dying from hoof and knife disease. Ha!"

"I've read that Ute Indians once lived all over much of Colorado, and around here."

"True, in the Garden of the Gods area and around Manitou especially because of the mineral springs there and the reason we now have Ute Pass so named for them. Sometimes their arrowheads and pieces of broken pottery are found by collectors. But long before them, so I'm told, the cliff ruins near Manitou were once of an ancient group known as Anasazi. The ruins suggest they lived there permanently, but the Yutas as we call Utes didn't."

"Why do you think?"

"Because of the herds of buffalos that once used Ute Pass in summers to get up higher where its cooler and the grasses are greener, then down again in the winter to move back out onto the plains. Since buffalos were their main source of food the Yutas followed them up and down, so they never stayed long in any one place. And in fact, it's known that buffalo trails in the Pass can still be seen in some places. I haven't seen them myself but the trail is said to be about fifteen inches wide and four inches deep."

"That suggests the herd walked in single file in those places where the Pass is narrow and steep. They obviously couldn't walk around in mass as they do out on the plains, but let's backtrack here a bit to some of the things you said."

"Oh! What did I say?"

"You said your sister was twenty-three years-old, and two years older than you."

"Yes! I said that."

"Then three years ago you were twenty-one."

"Yes! So?"

"I'm not too good in arithmetic, Sally," Ken grinned to speak her first name, "but now you must be, let's see..." said with a finger to his temple in pretense thinking, "you must be...."

"I'm twenty-four." Sally laughed to interrupt his very obvious pretense posturing to figure out something so simple to compute.

"Well, as a general rule, men don't like to be younger than the women they ask out for dinners. I'm twenty-six and I would like to have dinner with you this evening so we can talk some more. May we?" Ken smiled, and Sally couldn't help to not smile back about his crafty roundabout way to know her age in order to ask for a dinner date.

"We have house rules here about female employees socializing with male guests. There are sometimes the unfortunate damsel-in-distress kinds of situations that can happen. But yes, I would enjoy having dinner with you."

"Okay, right on. That's jolly good!" he said in English English...how about seven?"

• • • •

Ken Stanley and Sally Ruth liked one another from the moment they first saw one another and began talking when all he said to her from the start was a simple "hello," but just then Sally had need to break away from their engaging conversation when another person showed up at the desk to inquire about a room.

"Excuse me," Sally apologized gracefully to Ken but quickly added: "We have a very nice dining room here with a very good menu. It opens at six and closes at ten. There is a waiting area just inside with comfortable chairs to sit. Let's meet there, and if you haven't yet had one in this part of the country you might enjoy an elk steak...some say better than beef...or a roasted prairie chicken, also very tasty."

"If they are as good as English partridges I'll give one a try." He grinned.

Ken went up to his room on a hydraulic elevator to freshen up a bit, and to take a long look at the snow-covered Rockies and Pike's Peak from his room balcony, then back down and with a wave to Sally still at the registration desk went outside still early in the sunny mid-May fresh air afternoon. Ken needed to buy a horse to ride and to carry his butterfly net and associated paraphernalia. He, too, needed a rifle for subsistence hunting when out on his own and a revolver for self-defense if ever needed. He just heard about renegade Indians still about.

[Aboriginal Native Americans could be friendly to Anglo-Americans when it behooved them to barter animal hides for trade goods and such but turn on one in a minute with no seemingly good reason and resort to thievery, murder, and abductions of women and children for ransom. By the 1880s most Ute Indians in the region had been moved onto the Uncompahgre and the Uintah Indian Reservations in Utah though pioneer settlers living in more remote areas harbored fears of those still hiding out to avoid capture. Now and then one or more of them were seen still living in the wild in well-hidden wikiups.]

In a general merchandise store Ken found several handguns and long rifles for sale. He liked and bought a lever action .44-40 caliber 1873 Winchester rifle and a Colt Frontier .44-40 revolver so that both weapons could use the same cartridges. At a stable Ken found a two year-old roan gelding for sale named Prince and it being advertised as gentle and easy to ride sold Ken to buy it along with a saddle, blanket, halter and reins, and fortunately a saddle holster for a rifle.

Ken took the roan to pasture in the hotel's adjacent field and stable, then to ride it the next several days to investigate the Front Range of the Rockies for any Parnassian butterflies, if there, though he expected it more likely to find them up through Ute Pass to higher elevations and on rocky talus slopes where their *Sedum lanceolatum* host plants grow.

On return to the hotel lobby, and luckily, Ken saw Sally Ruth still working the Registration Desk. "Hello" he called out when then the two conversed a bit on his shopping for firearms and a horse to ride.

"What are your plans after leaving here next week?"

"I want to get up into higher elevations, maybe up to ten thousand feet where Parnassians may already be sipping on flower nectars, and maybe happily mating already." Ken grinned in the saying and as expected, Sally blushed a bit to hear it said. Yet, the comment was made in truth and for a good reason since it was to his needs in Colorado to find both virgin and non-virgin females though, too, said with intent to help get past any awkwardness between them, if need be, to get better acquainted and into more familiar and less formal conversations with questionable words.

"Where do you want to look for them?"

"Up around Green Mountain Falls and above where at this time of year there should be some already flying, but wherever found I need to collect a good number of just-emerged virgins, and then others a day later after losing their innocence. It doesn't take long with them." Ken grinned. "The females mate as soon as flying and to collect virgins they must be caught just when emerging. Moreover, it's the peculiar anatomy of female Apollos in need of further study."

"What's so peculiar about that?" Sally asked innocently and unsuspecting of the coming answer.

"Well if you want to know the whole truth of it…it's the peculiarity of their, well, their lady parts."

"Oh! There!"

"Yep! There."

"I didn't need to know anything about that." Sally admitted, still with a blush. "But now that you've got me curious tell me, how do you know if a female butterfly is a virgin? Do you ask her? And what if she doesn't want to tell?" Sally grinned, and Ken likewise in return. The ice was breaking for more familiarity in conversations between them.

"There is no need to ask. After a male and his lady friend do their…well…do their mating thing he deposits a wax-like version of a chastity belt, a so-called sphragis or a mating plug over her…her lady part…so that another male can't also fertilize her eggs, or try and can't. Simply, male number one wants only his caterpillars to hatch and not those of another. Moreover, to further answer your question, females that don't have mating plugs are logically assumed to be virgins. No need to ask, just look, sort of like being a butterfly gynecologist," Ken laughed, "and the only way to identify Parnassian species with any measure of certainty is to look closely at the female's lady parts. So now you know."

"Well, thanks for telling me!" Sally remarked though still with a modest blush. Ken smiled within to have further explained all just said, and being another step establishing more familiarity between them in things discussed.

"Whichever male is or was the lucky one," Ken continued, "doesn't matter to me as I'm not a geneticist to care much about which male fathered which brood of caterpillars, but where I can find them I would like to know after hatching how far young caterpillars may range from one host plant to the next when feeding. Caterpillars of some species will completely eat all of the leaves on a plant before moving on in search of another. I would like to know how long Parnassians live as caterpillars before pupating and just in general anything of interest about their life habits. I just like to know about such kinds of things of butterflies, and moths."

"You seem obsessed with them to want to know it all." Sally grinned, as did Ken in response.

"By the way," Sally added, "I'm glad you're here to tell you that I need to work a bit later this evening. Let's have dinner at eight."

• • • •

It was then five and Ken had a three hour time period to shower, to rest awhile, and to change into dressier clothes with a coat and tie (**Fig. 1**) for the much looked-forward to dinner date. He correctly anticipated that Sally would dress smartly for the occasion but more than expected when he saw her that like a butterfly damsel had metamorphosed from a uniformed desk clerk into a stunningly dressed *mademoiselle la belle dame*. She was a belle of the ball and as if she had just stepped from off a fashion cover of *Le Journal des Modes*. Sally had coiffured her curly brown hair (**Fig. 2**) up onto the top of her head and held in place with a head-band decorated with dainty flowers. Especially alluring of her to see, Sally's off-the-shoulder dress revealed sensual shoulders and a delicate neckline.

"Oh me, right on!" Ken exclaimed to himself on seeing Sally Ruth dressed as lovely as now seeing her. "Lucky me!" he said to himself again. The two vacated to a dinner table lit with candles and entertained by the romantically appealing dining room piano and violin music, almost as if just for them. While awaiting mutual orders of roast prairie chickens Sally, curious to know, asked how he had travelled so far to come to Colorado all the way from far away England.

"Well, it was a long voyage across the Atlantic on a sixty foot schooner flying an American flag, and well-rigged with all of its many jibs, staysails, mainsails and the towering top sails. We made two two-day stops in the Canaries off the west coast of Africa and in the Bahamas in the Caribbean, then eventually in New York City at a dock on the Erie Canal. From there for two days I travelled mostly on the Union Pacific Railroad into Denver and then here on the Colorado Midland. I plan to stay here until next week and then at least another two weeks in Green Mountain Falls."

"Why not longer?"

"The museum where I work wants all of the Apollo butterflies that I can collect back as soon as possible while they are still in relatively good condition. Two weeks up in the Green Mountain Falls valley and surrounding peaks should be sufficient time to collect enough. They are generally high-altitude forms and, interestingly, all the way up to snow lines, which is why Parnassian butterflies are sometimes known as snow butterflies of the mountains."

"Then I should tell you that I too will be moving to Green Mountain Falls next week to be concierge at the new Green Mountain Falls Hotel though I'm told that now it's only known as The Hotel. I've not yet been there to see it but I'm told by General Palmer who recommended me for the job, that it's a grand three story Victorian era structure with seventy rooms and some up high in gables (**Fig. 4.** 1893).

The hotel also has a large dining room, parlor, game room and dancing floor for waltzes and square dances. There is even a smoking room for gentlemen."

"It all sounds exciting. I want to see it myself when I get there but I won't need the smoking room," he laughed, "but we can try out the dance floor if you'd like." He grinned.

"That would be fun." Sally smiled. "I love square dances with all the whirls and twirls, promenades, sashays and do-si-does and such. General Palmer also told me that all three floors have full length verandas looking out across the lake and town, and the new Midland railroad station. He says the few people who now live the year-around in Green Mountain Falls [only about forty in the late 1880s] aren't enough to meet all of the hotel's needs for employees such as porters, waiters and waitresses, chamber maids and janitors, chefs and bus boys and the likes who will move in from afar.

"I'm told," Sally continued, "that many guests are expected to arrive on horseback likely meaning the need of a corral, barn and stable hands. People who arrive on trains may want to ride horses while in town. I love to ride them myself. The hotel's omnibuses will need horses and drivers.

"I'm excited to be working in the new Green Mountain Hotel expected to rival the ornate Ramona Hotel in nearby Cascade with its Byzantine dome with one hundred bedrooms, and nearby to it the many-gabled Cascade House Hotel. Further down the road are the many tourist facilities in Colorado City, Manitou and Colorado Springs, and further up is the Woodland Park Hotel. I hear that it has forty-two bedrooms, a large dining room served by two kitchens, and two parlors. Also up in Divide at the head of Ute Pass is the new Crest Hotel with fifteen guest rooms. There, too, I understand are boarding houses for long-time stays."

[The valley of Green Mountain Falls was first ranched by George Howard in 1881 then sold to W.J. Foster in 1887 to build there a summer resort. He gave the town its name when the Colorado Midland Railroad was built through the valley and the town with a station. All of it enjoyed great success from the start with the opening of the hotel in May, 1889. The lake was excavated; the island for a gazebo was built; the streets were laid out; and tent cabins were erected renting from $4 to $7 a week. All had wood floors, canvas tops and each a pot-bellied stove, beds and a table and chairs. There is boating and fishing in the lake, and hiking trails up along the water falls in the area, as well as baseball games, Saturday night square dances and the concerts by the Colorado Midland Band.]

"That's exciting to hear about it all and which raises the possibility of us traveling together next week to get there."

"That would be fun and you would have a place to stay in one of the tent cabins. I'll have private quarters in the hotel."

"A tent is good enough for me. I'm accustomed to sleeping in them or out under the stars." Both laughed, and with more laughter about one thing and another over the delightful two hour dinner sitting opposite and listening to the romantic music, during which both got to know one another and over time more and more familiar and in the private and personal things talked about.

Ken Stanley spent the next two days riding his horse Prince a few miles east of Colorado Springs out along the Front Range of the Rockies looking for *Sedum lanceolatum* host plants for Rocky Mountain Apollos but, regretfully, saw none of either. All yet that Ken had seen, ever, of any Apollos were the mounted specimens in the British Museum, those of his employer Edward

Doubleday who in 1847 had used them to name and describe the *Parnassius smintheus* species with its one type specimen and several paratypes that further authenticated the description and naming of a new butterfly species.

[The Greek name *smintheus* being the surname of *Apollo Smintheus* is first mentioned in Homer's *Ilias* (Iliad) I, 39, where "The old man, afraid, prayed to Lord Apollo," and elsewhere is written of the "mighty Lord of Tenedos, Sminthean (Smintheus) Apollo." Such source names are the whys of the Rocky Mountain Parnassians being given the specific Greek name, *Smintheus*, and the group of several species being called "Apollos."]

Ken Stanley wasn't new to butterfly biology, ecology, histories and nomenclatures as when a young teenager he was obsessed with butterflies and chased after them with a net and with the stumbling obstacles encountered of fences, creeks, rocks and logs, and when running pell-mell through gardens and farm fields and over and through meadows and marshes and along the edges of woods where plenty of poison sumac, thorn bushes, cactuses and sticky thistles grew. He too was an avid reader of the literature on the many families and species of butterflies. Ken studied Doubleday's treatise *The Genera of Diurnal Lepidoptera Comprising their Genetic Characters*, as well as his lengthy *List of the Specimens of Lepidopterous Insects in the Collections of the British Museum.* Just ten years earlier than Doubleday the American Ferdinand Heinrich Hermann Strecker published to the acclaim by collectors his monumental *Butterflies and Moths of North America* including 399 new species and 150 subspecies. The three works studied were Bibles of information that Ken read, but there were others.

He prepared for his work in the American States perusing through William Henry Edwards' early editions of *The Butterflies of North America* with 104 color Plates and descriptions through the 1860s, 1870s, and those already published through much of the 1880s of more than five hundred pages. Much read too was Frenchman Jean Baptiste Boisduval's *General History and Illustrations of the Lepidoptera and Caterpillars of Northern America* published in 1837 ten years before Edward Doubleday's Rocky Mountain Apollo studies. But far and away the collecting of butterflies as by Ken, and postage stamps by others were the two most popular hobbies worldwide but not to forget fossils, seashells and pressed flowers.

• • • •

On the two evenings after returning to the Antlers, Ken and Sally dined together a second and third time; one night relishing a recommended elk steak and the other a fried lake trout, also delicious, and each evening listening to romantic piano and violin music. During each long dinner date sitting close and opposite one another with enjoyable togetherness, there grew levels of attraction and fondness of one for the other as new found friends.

[English Poet John Keats wrote of two young people fast falling in love. "They could not together be without some stir of heart. / They could not sit at meals but feel how well it soothed each to be with the other. / They could not, sure, beneath the same roof sleep, but to each other dream and nightly weep. / With every morn their love grew tenderer / With every eve deeper and tenderer still."]

The Play

The five principal characters stood about mingling with General Palmer and his dignitary guests being William S. Jackson of the Denver and Rio Grande Railway; James J. Hagerman, a major stockholder in the First National Bank; Joel Adison Hayes, Jr. then co-owner of the Colorado Midland Railway; Edwin Eaton, President of the Colorado Savings Bank, and the German Count, James M. Pourtales, who was owner of the Broadmoor Dairy Farm [later of the Broadmoor Hotel and gardens] and the Cheyeene Lake Land Development Company.

The only singer was soprano Maiden Mary and to Ken's good luck and quite by chance made eye-contact with her. They exchanged opportunistic smiles though she knew him not. Ken however remembered her well when hearing her to sing in the same *King Charles the Second* play in London's Royal Opera House. Not only did Mary have a beautiful voice she like Sally was quite pretty and about the same age.

The other four of the five characters were Captain Copp, a former sailor and now owner of the tavern named "The Grand Admiral" where his niece, Mary, lived upstairs and who King Charles the Second wanted to meet and get to know though with immoral and lustful thoughts despite his being married to the Queen. The third main character was Lady Clara, also a royal, who the fourth main character, the scoundrel Lord Rochester, wanted to marry. Number five in the Play was the King's page, Edward, who loved Mary and it being through Edward that King Charles had heard about living at the tavern.

Off stage in the adjoining dining room there sat at tables a number of local bit-players filling in and acting as noisy drunken sailors and to be heard only as raucous background tavern noise and being out of sight.

Sally sat with hotel guest and new friend, Ken, on front row seats reserved especially for her by General Palmer. The city dignitaries and business friend guests of General Palmer also had front row seats and in the several rows behind there sat the many guests in the fully-filled hotel and others of the large hotel staff.

The lobby's curtains were closed to dim it and as the play started the overhead gas lights dimmed to further darken the room. The makeshift stage by the front desk was lit, and when on cue the five main characters reentered the lobby to the audience's applause and in theatrical tradition the three men made bows right and left and the two girls held their dresses, bent their knees, and curtsied politely to the audience and to another round of applause.

In Act One, Lady Clara took center stage with the scoundrel, Lord Rochester, and throughout the Act expressed his love for Lady Clara, wanting to marry her though also wanting to make-out with maiden Mary, the knave that he was. Maiden Mary didn't come on stage until Act Two.

In Act Two, the story involved adventures of sweet Mary and her sour-tempered uncle, Captain Copp, caught up in the plots and, though funny, the twisted escapades of Lord Rochester, King Charles the Second, and the King's page, Edward, who loved Mary.

ACT TWO
Scene One

Captain Copp's tavern "The Grand Admiral."
Mary comes on stage and gives her opening
monologue. Heard from noisy voices within the
tavern but not seen, drunken off-stage sailors call
out loudly: Wine! Wine! Barmaid more wine!
(Much laughter by the hotel audience).

Mary (forlornly): What noises drunken sailors make in the barroom. I should like to take a peep at them but my uncle forbids me to show myself in the public rooms. He brings me up more like a young lady than a niece of the tavern keeper.

What a tiresome long day! I wonder what can keep my singing teacher away. For three days he has not been here to give me a lesson...and he was just teaching me a pretty song, too...all about love. I'll try (attempts to sing). No, I can't...it's all out of my head...well so much the better!

Mary paced the stage emoting despairingly, then at last does sing, and as she started, and as Ken remembered to hear such a beautiful soprano voice, slipped his hand into Sally's feeling the warmth and softness of it for the first time, and testing her response to his bold attention. Sally didn't object, and except for occasions of applause, and when the lights came up for intermissions, the two held hands the remainder of the play, and his squeezes being silent forms of conversation "in tune" with certain lines in the play.

> Oh! Not when other eyes may read
> My heart upon my sleeve.
> Oh! Not when other ears can hear,
> Dare I speak of love.

At the "dare I speak of love" Ken squeezed Sally's hand gently. She squeezed back though unaware of his thoughts and the reason(s) for them. Mary continues to sing in her beautiful, lyrical, soprano voice.

> But when the stars rise from the sea,
> Oh then I think of thee, dear love!
> Oh then I think of thee.

Ken squeezed again to the words "I think of thee, dear love," and with another timely squeeze Sally began to suspect that Ken was speaking to her through his squeezes synchronized with words to the song. Had he just told her he loved her? Had he just called her "dear love?" Dare she squeeze back? Sally wondered, and Mary continued to sing.

When o'er the olives of the dell
The silent moonlight falls,
And when upon the rose,
Oh then I think of thee, dear love,
Oh then I think of thee.

Ken squeezed again to "I think of thee, dear love." Sally's heart raced at his signal that she was "dear love." Yes! It had to be. His squeezes coincident with certain words must mean he loves her. Sally placed her disengaged hand across her neckline lest Ken see her glow. She tried to constrain mutual feelings but it was all for naught. Sally squeezed back in response to say the same.

Sally found concentration on the play difficult when half-listening and half-dreaming. She sat absorbed in her own romantic thoughts of the man beside her, and by his responsive squeezes saying that he loved her. Words through timely squeezes communicated messages of fond affections though not one word was said aloud. The play continued.

Rochester: I must see this barmaid named Mary...I hear she is devilishly pretty.

Ken squeezed to tell Sally that she, too, was "devilishly pretty." Sally almost laughed aloud knowing that she could be "devilishly impish" when it behooved her. Now she learned she was "devilishly pretty." Sally looked at Ken and wrinkled her nose, then diverted her eyes back to the play. King Charles entered.

Rochester: (assuming a serious air): I must beg your majesty to excuse me early. I have an engagement of an important nature.

Charles: Wither does this engagement take place?

Rochester: At the tavern The Grand Admiral. I'll see there a girl I'm told is as beautiful as an angel.

Ken squeezed to say that Sally too is "as beautiful as an angel." His signals in lieu of words were unquestionable. Sally responded with a squeeze of acknowledgment to the compliment then whispered "thank you" to him. Ken now knew for certain that his messages were getting through.

The comedic escapades of King Charles the Second escalated through the play for another hour to intermittent bursts of laughter and applause as actors entered, emoted lines, and exited. In the following ending Act Three, suspicious Captain Copp catches on to the King's wants to seduce his niece, then with a shotgun chases after him and the King (all this time incognito and unrecognized as to who he is) runs back to Buckingham Palace and hides within. Captain Copp runs up and down the hallways and from one room to another trying to find him. The play in its entirety was worthy of the raves and applauses by all in the lobby audience. At times in the Play "Bravos" were cried out. The play drew to a close and the lights came up again but this time further emoted by Captain Copp and King Charles.

Captain Copp: So here we are all safe in port after all of our shenanigans…and with the betrothals of Lady Clara to Lord Rochester and maiden Mary to the King's page, Edward.

King Charles: Let me particularly enjoin all present here today the most profound secrecy in regard to our whimsical tomfoolery. The world is never to know the escapades of the English monarchy and those especially here in Little London. [The audience laughed and applauded at the Little London comment.] I ask for honor among you today to keep this secret quiet. Mum's the word from this time on.

On cue, the other three in the cast returned to the stage and all five together made bows left and right in appreciation of the thunderous applause. The cast then with all hands held took one last long bow in unison to then walk off the stage to shake hands with General Palmer in appreciation of his generosity for all of the hotel's services provided without costs. Ken and Sally squeezed hands one last time, and to Ken's good luck managed to make another chance eye contact with the Mary actress and to exchange smiles, though as said she knew him not but he remembered her well.

Later when in the hotel barroom with time at last to be alone and with a drink each, Ken asked: "So how did you like the play and the soprano's singing?"

"I loved it all, and Mary is a very good singer."

"Do you per chance sing?" Ken asked out of curiosity.

"If you're thinking like Mary, then forget it. I don't know an 'A' from a 'K.'" Sally laughed.

"Well, if you don't know the key of 'A' and you can't reach as high as a 'K' then I must guess that you don't sing."

"I can hum though...to myself." Both laughed and as both knew of it all to be just kidding around.

"What about the Play? Did you like it?"

"Of course I liked it! It was very funny. It made Lord Rochester to be quite the scoundrel that he was, didn't it, but maybe more so King Charles the lothario that he was when trying to seduce Mary while being married to the queen."

"Well what you may think to the contrary, virtues and inhibitions break down behind closed doors and beneath bed sheets, and unquestionably with Royals. Queens relieve their boredom and pent-up urges with pages and stable grooms and kings with chambermaids and nannies. Even beneath their habits and cloth, priests and nuns are still human with all the urges, and despite vows of celibacy may well slip up, transgress and go astray. [Sally blushed to hear of such things.] History reveals that King Charles the Second had thirteen love affairs and…." Sally interrupted and gasped: "Thirteen! Heavens! I didn't know Royals had one affair."

"Well, falling in love with someone one shouldn't is what must be I rather think a common occurrence wherever and with whomever and not fall to the temptations of romantic affairs, even with Royalty. If you knew of them I suspect Little London right here in Colorado is rife with love affairs of one kind or another."

"Must be like *Old* London…I'm just guessing." Sally said to poke a bit of fun at Ken who grinned by the remark and implication. "How long do affairs last…to *your* knowledge?" She asked as if he *did* know. But the asking such suggested that Sally was quickly adopting a level of familiarity between them more than just teasing quips and casual repartee.

"Not from *my* experience." Ken grinned, "I wouldn't know of such, but I'm guessing that just a one-night or even a one hour kind of affair happens every day down in Old Colorado [pioneer era Colorado City known for its brothels]." Ken grinned again. "I suppose affairs can last for days, weeks, or months. Some may last for years or a lifetime. Who knows except only those involved…I'm just guessing however." Ken grinned.

"What if we bug out of here for the rest of the day," Sally asked. "We can catch a horse car for Colorado City and Manitou and I can show you around the Old City area. I always like to window shop when there and its early enough that we can go see Rainbow Falls near Manitou, sometimes called Ute Falls. It's a pretty place. I like waterfalls."

"Me too! Let's go!"

"Then wait here while I change into something else. The horse-drawn trolleys have no windows and it can get breezy at times in afternoons. Bonnets that can be tied are better to wear than hats that can blow away despite hat pins." Sally laughed. "Do you chew and spit?" She asked casually with a teasing grin.

"No! Of course not! Why ask?"

"Men who chew and spit are asked to sit on the down-wind sides of horse cars. Ha!"

The two took a courtesy omnibus ride to the Colorado Springs passenger station on East Pike's Peak Avenue, then for five cents each rode to Colorado City and adjacent Manitou. And now almost always hand-in-hand they walked down the street fronting on the shopping strip with its plethora of stores such as art galleries, boutiques, curio shops, restaurants, and such, but also saloons and brothels [the so-called fleshpots] not permitted in Colorado Springs. Here and there were the needs to step around trash as the streets were unclean despite the town's popularity to tourists.

"Yuk!" Sally exclaimed where in one spot some smelly rotting garbage was mixed in with the trash.

When window shopping through the front of an art gallery Ken's attention was drawn to a picture propped up on an easel known to him once seen in London's Royal Academy of Art, and being a work of art by John William Waterhouse, a popular English artist of the time. They walked inside, and on looking Ken remarked: "Yes! It's a print of his 'A Mermaid' picture. Sexy, isn't she?"

"Yes, but she should be wearing a top of some kind."

"You could close your eyes and not look." Ken laughed. "Have you ever seen a picture of a mermaid wearing clothes?"

"Well, no, but maybe they should be."

"In case you didn't know, nude paintings are much loved works of classical art and even as puritanical as is Queen Victoria she enjoys such and I hear she commissions nude paintings as gifts to Prince Albert and he for her. She once said 'Shame on you who think ill of them.' World museums are famous for nude sculptures of one kind or another and especially where seen are those of Greek and Roman goddesses as Venus de Milo and Aphrodite, and of naked Gods such as Apollo and David showing up front the best of them looking right back at you." Ken said in jest and Sally blushed to think such.

"Nude paintings and statues," Ken continued, "are art if for nothing more than the sake of art, and nudity *can* acquire respectability. Haven't you ever seen a naked statue?"

"Well, yes, one time in a Chicago art museum in Grant Park. It was a replica of a Greek marble called the Barberina Faun. My sister Sue looked and giggled, but I turned my head. I didn't want people to see me looking."

"I suspect you looked anyway and saw in awe what looked back at you." Ken grinned.

"I admit to a peak, but a girl can't help where she looks, can she?"

"I guess not, nor men, but know that Nudes are works of art, and back in ancient times bare breasts were stylish, and period artists paint accurate to the times. Even today there are parts of the world, in the South Pacific and in dark Africa and in the Australian outback for examples, and even in Bali where women wear nothing above their waists."

"Well, they should, at least if out in public." Sally laughed.

"As interesting as it may seem," Ken continued to press his point and be said to tease Sally all the more, "some of the most erotic of fantasy art are paintings of voluptuous little faeries so dainty and small they could sit on toadstools and wear bluebells and foxgloves for hats, even thimbles, and be draped with their own hair, or clothed in moon mist or draped in spider silk and be so translucent to add little to nothing to propriety. Surely you've seen pictures of them and right through whatever they're wearing."

"In story books."

"Then there you are to have seen of such!" Ken grinned. Sally blushed and in play slapped him on his arm. "Oh hush!" she said. Good-humored bantering and light-hearted chit-chat back and forth was fast becoming every opportunity for it fun. Ken delighted in it to tease and to carry on with her and she with him.

• • • •

The next day was a Sunday and for Sally a day off from work. Plans were made to ride horses together out into flatter areas along the eastern edge of the Front Range of the Rockies south of Colorado Springs to look for meadows in bloom. Ken hoped in them to find specimens of the Rocky Mountain Apollos already in flight. He saddled Prince and a horse from the hotel stable for Sally while she dressed for the occasion.

Too, he packed a butterfly net and a shoulder bag with an assortment of accessory collecting equipment along with a canvas tarp in case of an afternoon shower common to happen when on warmer days moisture-laden thermals cool in height, cloud over, and precipitate. At Sally's request the hotel chef made sandwich lunches for them.

When Sally appeared dressed for the occasion with ruffled pantalets beneath an ankle-length dress to sit astride saddles, she was pretty to see wearing a calico bonnet with colorful bows, ribbons and decorative lace. Moreover, Sally's waistline drawn in tightly by a belt accentuated the sensual hourglass curvatures of what of her lay beneath.

"Wow!" he exclaimed to himself. "Pretty!" he said aloud to Sally who smiled and replied with a "thank you" comment and a blush.

Sally knew how to ride horses. She was an equestrian good at it, though she knew nothing about netting butterflies. When seeing the insect net strapped across the pommel of Ken's saddle, she asked: "Do you think you might collect an Apollo today?"

"I hope so, but if we see a butterfly of any kind I can show you how to catch one."

"I'm okay with that!" Then out of curiosity Sally casually asked: "Do you say 'okay' in England?"

"Yes, but also 'right on,' and if said at the right moment for its meaning, 'right-on' means the same thing, and an emphatic 'blimy' exclamation followed by an emphasized 'right on' comment is a really meaningful 'okay." Ken laughed.

"Right on!" Sally responded with a rather good imitating attempt to sound English.

"Sally Ruth was amusing and quite pretty. Her brown hair and eyes were most appealing. Every girl should be so lucky and Sally was more than just lucky. She was blessed. She stood tall, slender and statuesque and quite charming in her mannerisms and in her ways of saying things and in carrying on amusing conversations. Sally, obviously, was from a good circle of well-to-do family and friends. She was smart and obviously well educated, and certainly well-liked by fellow employees in the Antlers. There was little doubt of it by anyone knowing of Sally's being a favorite of General Palmer—Sally has said he was like a father to her—and guests in and out of the hotel often commented on what a pleasant and friendly desk clerk as was Sally Ruth.

> [Sally Ruth could well have been the inspiration to that penned by the classical Romanticists of Ken's Victorian era England. In the words of William Wordsworth, Sally was a "phantom of delight." She was Sir Walter Scott's The Lady of the Lake "with locks flung back and lips apart / Like some monument of Grecian art / A Nymph, a Naiad, or a Grace / Of no finer form or lovelier face. Sally could well have been William Blake's inspiration, like Ken's thoughts, that women were "Works of God." Such was Sally so blessed.]

Not long into their horseback ride, a meadow in full bloom was seen in the near distance and for the fun of it the two raced off together to get there quickly in an easy loping cantor comfortable for horse and rider. Both liked the speed of a fast horse and some of Sally's curls beneath her bonnet swirled about her face and tickled her nose. Riding together was fun, and more so when on other occasions Sally rode double behind Ken with her arms wrapped around his waist though, maybe, a little tighter than necessary.

Once into the middle of the meadow and seen all around were the "flowers of the month." April showers had brought on May flowers in resplendent displays not only of their varied colors but also the forms that nature gives them such as Indian Paint Brushes, Bluebonnets, and Wine Cups that normally give way to June's pink and yellow Primroses and purple Verbenas and Phlox. But already there were the beginnings of summer's yellow sunflowers interspersed with white daises and Prickle Poppies. All brightened up the landscape to lighten one's heart to see them, added to by the pleasures of it all when one also inhales the intoxicating fragrances of wild flowers, and not the least to it all is to hear the melodious singing of passerine songbirds. One's soul revels in it all. Somewhere off in the near distance the very best of all singers, a Mockingbird sang.

On this day being already much warmer in the afternoon sun, honey bees and bumble bees buzzed about laden with yellow flower pollen. Dragonflies were seen here and there. In riding along and when frightened by their nearity a cottontail scampered off, and in another place a covey of quail flew off in all directions in a burst of flight. Just ahead about a rocky outcrop a patch of red and yellow flowers turned out to be Sedum Stonecrops being the food plants of Apollo caterpillars. The two dismounted and when down on their hands and knees raked though the leaf litter and loose soil beneath in search for overwintering pupae that may just now be emerging as adults.

"Nope!" Ken lamented. However, butterflies of other species were about in flight and a short distance away Ken spotted a Monarch feeding on milkweed nectar.

"Do you want to catch a butterfly?" He asked.

"Yes! Can I?"

"Give it a try. Do you see that orange-colored butterfly feeding on milkweeds?"

"What kind is it?"

"It's a Monarch which is found in both the Americas and in England. It's one I want to send back for comparisons of morphological differences between the two populations. There might be differences in wing shapes and venation and such."

Ken showed Sally how to take swings at butterflies with the net wide open. Then said: "If you catch a butterfly, quickly flip the net over on its self to trap it inside. It will flutter around trying to escape but can't, and then I'll show you how to get it out."

For the first time in all twenty-four years of her young life, Sally was going to catch a butterfly, or try at least and as instructed approached the Monarch slowly to not scare it and with the net held out at arm's length took a swing at it. *Voilà*, she caught it, and quickly as instructed turned the net over onto itself to trap it inside.

"Look Ken. I got it." Sally proudly remarked with glee to have caught a butterfly on her first attempt.

"I saw you catch it, and it was a Jolly good show!" Ken called out, but unseen for the moment by its small size and mixed in with broken-off Milkweed flower petals and leaves, Sally also netted a wingless wasp known as a "Cow Killer" because of its excruciating sting, and which it too had been innocently feeding on milkweed nectar.

But, then, much to Sally's surprise and with no thought given of what he'd do and did was through the net pinch the Monarch's thorax to kill it.

"Oh yuck! Why did you do that?"

"Monarchs are needed back in England for comparison studies, but did you think alive?"

"No. But I didn't know dead! Poor thing! What are you going to do? Mail it in an envelope?"

"No Silly! I'll send it by a carrier pigeon." Ken said tongue in cheek to poke fun at Sally.

"I didn't know pigeons could fly that far. How long would it take?" Naive Sally asked.

"I'm just messing with you." Ken admitted.

"I kind of thought you were!" Sally retorted.

"I kind of thought you kind of thought I was." He replied in response and laughed.

Ken retrieved the Monarch from the net and spread its wings to check it out for its sex and in an instant claimed "this is a male."

"How did you know that so fast?"

"Look closely on the upper sides of its hind wings, and down low in the middle of each you will see tiny black spots

(**Fig. 5**). Those are male scent glands which emit pheromones smelling much like milkweeds which are attractive to Monarch females and when a sexy little *demoiselle* of her ilk answers to his 'call of the wild' so to speak with a sexy flutter of her wings, it's then straight to business for both, and with no foreplay I might add." Sally blushed to hear of such said.

"The male and his lady friend then…well…'do it,' and I should add here that it's often a matter of robbing the cradle because most often the female has just emerged. Her wings may not yet even be dry, but she already smells nice with her cloud of pheromones that lured him in and when all is done he leaves and her impregnated. It's a love them leave them sort of story." Sally blushed again by all just heard.

To show her how to pack it Ken removed from a saddle bag a cigar box filled with cotton batting along with pieces of glassine paper precut into rectangular shapes of assorted sizes. He selected one befitting to the size of the Monarch and it being too fast for Sally to see exactly how done, folded the glassine twice over onto itself and its edges twice more to form it into the shape of a triangle envelope. "I'll put the Monarch inside (**Fig. 6**) between layers of cotton so it doesn't

get rattled around and damaged in the handling. My dictum is that one perfect specimen is better than any number of damaged ones."

To then poke a bit of fun at Sally of other (inane) things explained, Ken continued. "You know...just in case you've ever wondered about it...what butterflies and people do concerning procreation needs to keep their species ongoing, it's all explained in the Bible that after God created the heavens and the earth, and when late one night in the Garden of Eden...and out of idle curiosity with nothing else much to do...Adam peeked under Eve's fig leaf and saw in awe what he saw, to be poetic about it."

"Oh hush!" Sally interrupted. "That's sacrilegious."

"Well, you need to know what Milton once said about Eve as being the 'fairest of God's creations, the best of all His works.' Not only that, Blake described a woman's nakedness as being a 'Work of God.' That's why Adam was so awestruck to see what he saw in awe of what he saw...to be even more poetic about it...what Eve had beneath her fig leaf. But that's not the end of the story. What then followed when in the grip of unaccountable urges and drives they hardly understood, they too like the butterflies, well, 'did it.' And anyone curious enough to know more has to believe that what then happened was how and when Eve lost her innocence and how female butterflies get fertilized."

"You're just joshing me. I didn't read any of that in *my* Bible about Eve and butterflies. You need another version of yours to get your facts straight."

"Okay! I'm just kidding, but the *real* story is that God commanded Adam and Eve to 'be fruitful and unite as one' and it wasn't until after Cain, Abel and Seth were born that Adam and Eve figured out the why of their command to be fruitful when each of their sons was born exactly nine months after you know what. But do you want to know something that's also really true in the Bible...about butterflies that is?"

"What now?"

"That butterflies aren't mentioned anywhere in it. There are mentions of flies, ants, locusts, moths, and birds, and those which are clean or unclean to eat, but nowhere are butterflies mentioned. It must have been, I'm just guessing, that Moses didn't know about butterflies, and maybe because God forgot to mention them when Moses was told what to write in the Torah. And there is something else that Moses must have surely misunderstood about and got all wrong. He listed bats as one of the birds not to eat. And do you know that while much is written in both Testaments about countries like Israel, Palestine, Mesopotamia and Egypt, nowhere are countries mentioned as in Africa, America, and Australia, about gorillas, buffalos and kangaroos which Noah must not have known about to load two of each aboard his ark. And what about such animals as okapis and quaggas...and not to forget panda bears and Tasmanian devils…or even Tibetan Yetis." He grinned to add facetiously.

"Okay! Okay! Enough already" Sally said with a pretense frown and a playful slap across his arm. "You're a mental case about such dumb things. Someone must have dropped you on your head when you were little and if you need help for it wondrous things are being done in mental Institutions."

Both laughed at Sally's silly suggestion but such witty quipping back and forth was fast becoming fun, and on each occasion of it achieving more the intimacy and familiarity of things bantered in their budding new relationship.

Both then saw the wasp that looked more like a big red ant climb out of the net and drop to the ground (**Fig. 7**). Being a female of its kind it (she) was wingless and couldn't fly but like ants run fast. What they saw was a wasp of one of the so-called velvet ants because of their furry-like appearance and being easily mistaken for ants though much larger and more painful in their stings.

Ken knew of velvet ants because they also occur in England, and their kind being world-wide in distribution but only in warmer climates. One day in the Oare Marshes Nature Reserve in Kent, Ken saw one run hurriedly across his path and continue on for a long distance over obstacles as twigs, leaf litter, sticks and stones. It didn't seem bothered by Ken's following though it's never stopping made him think that it (she) knows where it's (she's) going and being anxious to get there in a hurry, but for what reason was a mystery.

A fellow entomologist along with Ken that day half-jokingly said that he had followed some of them far enough that if put all together "must be nigh onto twenty miles," he laughed. "I never saw them find anything or meet others of their kind and where they were going or what they were doing was a mystery to me. I never saw them end up anywhere." He laughed again.

[Female Velvet Ants are in a constant search for the burrows of ground nesting bumble bees or of other insects and the burrows of spiders. They lay their eggs on any larvae found inside which explains why they are on seemingly endless marches... being in search for egg hosts. Too, they have a habit of going down burrows head first, but backing out. Male velvet ants that have wings fly in search for females, being a *cherchez pour la femme* kind of evolutionary endeavor.]

Likewise, Ken and Sally followed the velvet ant to see where it (she) might be going but along the way and out of curiosity Sally poked it with a stick to stop it for a closer look and surprised to hear it squeak. For the fun of it, Sally poked the wasp again to hear another squeak sounding much alike a miniature buzz saw. "Funny" both exclaimed, and assumed in her wasp lingo to be saying "don't touch me or get stung."

[When predators such as lizards and frogs ignore the wasp's red color and buzz-like warning and catch one anyway to eat, they immediately spit them out because of the wasp's self-defense excruciating sting. It proves as well that when predators don't try to eat another, lessons had been learned from bad experiences.]

A few moments later they saw another Monarch feeding on a milkweed.

"Can I catch it too?"

"Yes! Of course! Go for it."

Once again Sally cautiously approached the Monarch with the net wide open and held full out at arm's length to net it but this time the butterfly flew and Sally had to chase after it with one hand holding up the hems of her dress and petticoat to dodge sticks and stones and plants with thorns.

"Cute!" Ken thought to himself. Sally was even more so when seen running fast in a long dress with hems lifted and catching the fast flying Monarch anyway with the good luck of a lucky good swing. "Jolly good!" Ken called out to her.

"What sex is this one?" Sally asked when back out of breath.

"Yuck!" She fretted again to see him pinch it.

"It's a female. See, there are no scent glands."

Sally's smile of pride grew into a wide grin of success in her want to net butterflies. It was fun for him to hear of such when Sally once mumbled "Drat" when the Monarch flew and she had to chase after it. On another occasion she muttered aloud a "Dang-it" when her dress snagged on a thorn bush. It was just plain fun for Ken to watch her in all things done together, and if their first meeting at the Antlers wasn't a case of love at first sight, it was close today, and now more so in what then quickly happened.

Off in the distance a bolt of lightning occurred and a rumble of thunder heard, and soon others and all with brighter lightning and louder claps of ear-splitting thunder as the rain storm neared. There were trees about to get beneath for some means of protection but during a lightning storm such wouldn't be a smart thing to do. The two tethered their horses to a sturdy low spreading Mountain Mahogany bush of dense and heavy hardwood branches so that they couldn't bolt and run if frightened by the louder and louder thunder. The winds picked up and by counting the seconds between bolts of lightning and claps of thunder they knew the storm would quickly be upon them and with the canvas tarpaulin Ken had wisely thought to bring they huddled close beneath it and up against the downwind side of another hardwood Mountain Mahogany shrub for additional protection.

The tarp further provided a good measure of welcomed warmth since the front of the storm became colder by its frigid downdrafts from high out of the clouds, and when the first of the hardest of rain hit it seemed as if all four winds from the south, north, east and west blew furiously at the same time. The countryside came afire with lightning strikes and the cracking sounds of thunder. Surely the Gods of all religions must have been angry at the world that afternoon to have produced such a tempest, and when the storm abated and finally stopped, Ken and Sally gave thanks to the Gods that they had survived such a furious storm, and embraced from a growing new friendship and fondness.

• • • •

That day was in the middle of May, 1889, and by the first of June Sally would start working as concierge of the new Hotel Green Mountain owned by the Green Mountain Falls Town and Improvement Company which then owned most of the town. The first of June meant Sally's having two free weeks to be with Ken, and he being anxious to work up in the higher elevations of the Green Mountain Falls valley when the Mountain Apollos would soon be flying if not already.

There was then and is now only one flight a year for Parnassian butterflies beginning by about mid-May to the first of

June and through to about the end of August or early September. The pupae then overwintered in cocoons and to not emerge until after the spring snows melted…being reason for the so-called Snow Butterflies of the Mountains…and with good reason Ken didn't want to miss collecting them when the Apollos first began emerging, flying and mating, then wait out the time their eggs would hatch and the first instar caterpillars do their thing to eat fast, grow fast, and to pupate beneath leaf litter or shallow in the soil.

Strangely for some butterfly species and not to forget moths, it would take days, weeks and months and sometimes as long as a year to live through all four stages of their life cycles, and with the adult stage lasting only a week or two or a month at most to mate, copulate, and lay their eggs. They would then die and even before the little caterpillars hatched to never know them, even if they cared. The laying of fertile eggs was their only purpose in life to keep their species going and then the adults so quickly dying.

The day of Ken's and Sally's leaving Colorado Springs from the Colorado Midland Railroad terminal, General Palmer, one of the founding fathers of the railroad, gave them tickets as a parting gift to Sally for her three years as a faithful employee in the General's Antlers hotel. Moreover, they were taken free to the station in a hotel horse-pulled omnibus and Ken's horse pulled along behind.

At the terminal the horse was loaded onto a covered stock car in with a load of cattle and other horses. However, sadly for Sally when told that the cattle were to be slaughtered for steaks at railroad stops with eating houses all the way to the mining camps at Cripple Creek and Leadville, and some at Green Mountain Falls for the new hotel there. The two had side-by-side seats in one of the new fifty-six seat Pullman first class coaches; the other two being less plush second class cars and before departure both were escorted by the conductor for a close look of the Baldwin ten-wheeler engine already ready to go.

That day to lead the way was a Baldwin built ten-wheeler 2-8-0 locomotive to pull the train and it being new and proudly sporting its engine number and with the rims on its eight drivers and two steering wheels painted white. [In its day between 1825 and 1975 the Pennsylvania based Baldwin Locomotive Works built 70,000 steam engines]. Its huge drivers were almost as tall as Sally and coupled behind were two Schenectady Company 2-8-0 ten-wheel helpers to assist the train up and over the steep grades of Ute Pass. The three locomotives ready to leave on the 11:15 am run west up Ute Pass sat idling and with their boilers already carrying the 160 pounds of steam pressure needed to get the train moving.

(Fig. 8).

[Early in the history of the Colorado Midland Railway it was realized that locomotives of exceptional power would be required to pull trains up the steep grades in Ute Pass and in places 4% grades being the hardest for any train to make. The

Baldwin and Schenectady 2-8-0 locomotives were reputed to be the largest of that wheel arrangement then made. Even so, and with a lead locomotive and its two helpers, one behind the tender to help pull and the other behind the caboose to push, the Ute Pass trains strained to get up the 3.5 % grades and slowing to walk speed at the highest 4% grades. Engineers described the walk speed climb up Ute Pass as "torturous."]

"This is Miss Ruth and Mr. Stanley" the conductor introduced them to the engineer and fireman of the lead engine. Polite "hellos" were cordially exchanged. "They will help you aboard and show you around inside the cab if you would like." The conductor and crew had been asked by General Palmer to personally give them a "first-class" tour of the train which included a "look-see" of the cab.

"Yes! Of course!" Ken answered. "We've never been inside one of these." Sally replied.

Now it isn't too easy to climb up into a locomotive cab higher than one stands though one can of course by using the ladders up in it. The engineer bent over to give Sally a helping hand the last step up. She was young and pretty and fashionably attired for the day when wearing a dress with puffed sleeves and a bustle with a colorful bow. He stood smitten and quickly learned that Sally had a most pleasing-to-hold soft hand when helping her in.

Once up and in (**Fig. 9**) and looking around at all of the levers, dials, gauges and wheels to run a steam engine, the first thing pointed to and explained was the steam gauge indicating 160 pounds of pressure but further said was to never let it go past the red line marked at 180. With a big grin, and being a man wearing a mustache with teeth in it, commented that "steam pressure more than the red line can make the boiler 'go boom.'" He laughed.

The fireman listening said, jokingly, "Yeah! A boiler blast could ruin *my* whole day to have to clean up the mess in here." He laughed but did say "there was a safety valve for anything more than 180 pounds of psi. An everyday mess is my job in here anyway is to keep clinkers out of the fire box and clean out all of the dead ash. That's hard, hot, backbreaking work, and not to mention that we firemen fill the water tanks in tenders when more is needed and these babies are real guzzlers. We don't get miles to the gallon. We get gallons to the mile, and we'll be using about thirty gallons per mile to get all the steam power needed to get up to the summit at Divide."

"You firemen must do a lot of the hard hot work in one of these." Ken commented.

"Yeah, and the worst of it is filling up the water tank in the cold of winter and in stormy weather when standing atop outside for the long time it takes to fill a five thousand gallon tank, and that after being hot and sweaty tending to the firebox. In my opinion nearly all of the illnesses we firemen suffer are for that reason…being hot and cold, hot and cold and in and out and in an out." He laughed while adding another few shovels of bituminous coal from the Vulcan coal mine in New Castle, being the hottest burning of other grades for the most power needed when steaming up Ute Pass. "And I'll be shoveling all needed from the twelve tons of it in the

Tender. That too is hard hot work." He said as he wiped more sweat from off his brow.

The engineer piped in to further explain that after leaving Manitou they *will* be needing all the steam power they can generate to get up to the summit. "That's a hard row to hoe as heavy as we are today and having to make some four percent grades in the steeper places. That's tough going. Even the three percent grades are hard to make." He grumbled, though with a smile and a wink at pretty Sally, who blushed.

"Yeah," the fireman piped in. "We'll slow to walk speed in the four percent stretches and if need be I'm the one having to get out to help push." He commented, jokingly.

[Just west of Manitou up Ute Pass to the summit was indeed the torturous 4% grade climbing 211 feet in each mile up to Cascade and west of Cascade was a maximum 3% grade. It was therefore the practice to make up a train in Manitou to the rated capacity of three engines on a 3% grade. Instead of reducing tonnage or adding another helper engine the westbound freight trains simply dragged down to walk speed on the five and one half miles of 4% grade, and struggled on uphill to Cascade and beyond. However, there were Midland trains in later years up to Divide with as many as five engines pulling and pushing as many as sixty-five ore cars.]

The engineer further commented that almost nowhere is there any dead level trackage or any grade less than sixteen feet a mile and "we may be sorry today to not have a third helper coupled in the middle to both push and pull. And if it rains today our drivers with little to no traction can spin when the rails are wet, and we may just have to sit until the sun comes out again." He joked with a wry grim looking back at

Ken and Sally and with another wink at Sally. "But once in Divide," he added, "we'll uncouple our two helpers, cut off their steam, and then go downhill awhile on the other side though then again up and over five other track levels and cross over the massive and very high wood trestle at Hagerman Pass. That's kind of scary to be up so high."

The fireman interjected to say: "he means so far down." All laughed.

The conductor listening in on all the banter then thought as a favor to give Ken and Sally a really "first-class" ride in keeping with General Palmer's request to do so, asked: "Would you like to ride here in the cab for the first miles to Manitou. It won't be anything fast and Manitou isn't far but you can see how one of these things work."

"Yes! Yes!" Both answered elated by the thought of it. The engineer sat taken aback a bit by the offer not previously discussed but being enamored with pretty Sally favored the idea to have her aboard in with him though the ride would be a short one. Moreover, her perfume was intoxicating, and Sally being aboard and being so pretty was a real plus.

> [Train conductors are in charge of all other crew employees, even of engineers who work under his or her direction. A train only goes after the conductor decides when ready and signals the engineers to start. He can even tell them when to stop and how long. However, engineers are in charge of the operation of locomotives but decisions of things to do are made *with* conductors for the safe operations and proper applications of railway rules and procedures.]

The engineer explained as a forewarning that "there will be a great deal of noise in the cab owing to the strain put upon the engine to get the train moving, and having a slow start to take up all the slack in the couplings. If we start with too much power we *will* spin the drivers." He laughed.

"We have ten cars today with the three fifty-five thousand pound coaches in which you will ride, plus three fifty thousand pound capacity gondola cars weighing twenty-two thousand pounds each, and each fully loaded with steel rail and bridge building timbers. There are two twenty-two thousand pound box cars with fifty thousand pound capacities and both fully loaded with furnishings for delivery in Divide still rebuilding from a fire there not long ago that destroyed the boarding houses used by Midland construction workers. Lastly are the thirty-two thousand pound stock car fully loaded today with your horse and a few others plus all the cattle, Mr. Stanley, and the thirty thousand pound caboose also called a 'way car' in which our two brakemen work to brake the cars and handle track switches.

"We will stop in Colorado City and Manitou to take on more passengers but from there on up to Cascade, Green Mountain Falls and Divide we hope there'll be no flag stops as when stopping and having to start uphill again is no fun. The time beyond Manitou as far as Divide depends much on the condition of the rails. In rainy and snowy weather, engine drivers slip badly to the curses of most engineers and me especially." He admitted, but with a grin. "Consequently little headway is made but thankful to our new Baldwin's eight drivers we have more traction now than the four drivers once used. In dry weather, traction is good all the way up but wheel slipping can happen in damp tunnels, and bad about that is if stalled in one the smoke inside is suffocating.

"At Cascade we will take on our first water and from there for the next two and a half mile run to Green Mountain Falls we can go a little faster where it's less steep, but only a little." He laughed. "We have orders today to meet train forty-nine in Green Mountain Falls coming down from Divide en route to Colorado Springs. If it's not there we'll sit on a siding to await its arrival and passage. Regulations provide that eastbound trains have right-of-track over those of the same class westbound which is us.

"Anytime a red light is on at a station it means for trains to stop for orders or stop for passengers but we usually stop anyway to let off passengers for stays in the new Green Mountain hotel and campgrounds. If there is no red light when going west it's a blessing of not having to stop and get started again uphill to Woodland Park and Divide.

"If you're interested when seeing it, engine forty-nine is also a Baldwin and though it's a year older than this one it's a heavier and a more powerful ten-wheeler. We are a one hundred and twenty-five thousand pounder with a tractive effort at twenty-two thousand pounds but number forty-nine weighs in at one hundred and fifty-four thousand pounds with a tractive effort of thirty-three thousand pounds. We have one hundred and sixty pounds of steam pressure. The forty-nine chugs along with one hundred and eighty pounds of steam. It's a real hog of an engine." He laughed again.

By the time all was said it was then 10:45 am and the conductor had to leave. The train was scheduled to depart in thirty minutes and he had to ensure that passengers already ticketed were properly seated and with tickets in hand. He punched each one with the almost always "welcome aboard" salutation but if a lady passenger sitting aisleside is young, pretty, and unencumbered, he might tarry to chat. But when all is done the conductor will wave a flag to signal the engineers to start moving.

For the fun of it during the short ten minute ride to Manitou, the engineer now all the more enamored with pretty Sally standing right next to him, let her pull down on the cord to blow the steam whistle, and when signaled in what sequences and durations of short and long blasts. As instructed, he would raise his arm and pretend to pull down on the cord and how long to hold it down, then raise his arm to stop it. He, too, would tend to the throttle and airbrakes and keep an eye on the steam pressure gauge along with the fireman. Today, though, both also kept an eye on Sally.

When ready to depart the Colorado Midland Colorado Springs depot, the engineer signaled Sally when to pull down on the whistle cord three times for five seconds each time. The two helper engines fully fired and hot to go tooted their whistles twice in return to acknowledge being "off brakes." Then with the Baldwin's and the two Schenectady engines up to full steam exhausting and hissing and with all three engines belching out dense clouds of black coal-fired smoke through their stacks started to roll.

Sally blew the whistle each time when told at all road crossings en route to Colorado City just three miles away but a slow ten minutes to get there. One long five second blow announced the train's arrival which Sally blew. A brief stop took on more passengers and through the town when just creeping along at walk speed, and when passing in front of the shops recently visited, Ken suddenly exclaimed in an excited voice: "Sally, look! Quick! Look in the gallery window. The mermaid picture is still there." "She's still topless." Sally joked. At the word "topless" overheard the fireman and engineer also looked.

Manitou was another three miles and another slow ten minutes away, but once there Sally's fun sorrowfully ended though to the welcomed relief to be out of the cab with its red hot firebox and boiler heat. They waved goodbyes to the crew and met the conductor again who ushered them to their assigned seats in the first class coach where, there, they rode hand in hand the remainder of the ride to Green Mountain Falls and along the way count all eight tunnels, then arrive at the depot next to the lake and near to the hotel.

(Fig. 10)

Baldwin locomotive number forty-nine had just arrived at the Green Mountain Falls train station, it being two small buildings next to the Gazebo Lake, and it being man-made and flowed into and filled from neighboring Catamount Creek. Crystal Creek flowed into Fountain Creek a bit further downhill. Engine forty-nine and all cars still had red hot wheels from the braking of all on a long downhill run and for the novelty of it smoking passengers lit cigarettes on them. One man fired up a dry twig to light his pipe.

A Hotel Green Mountain omnibus stood awaiting the expectation of both trains for the arrivals of guests though for the rest of the afternoon both went separate ways; Sally to the hotel to move into her personally assigned quarters with a bath and kitchenette, and Ken with his horse to the tent cabin campground and corral. However, both met at 7:00 for dinner together in the huge elaborate hotel dining room.

Sally's privately assigned quarters turned out better than anticipated, being quite well furnished with wall to wall carpeting and colorful wall hangings. Sally's windows with curtains and blinds looked out across the lake and its gazebo, and off in an uphill direction to the tent cabin campground where Ken would be staying. She looked but didn't see him.

Sally then heard a knock on her door and on answering, a porter handed her a note that was an invitation from the hotel builder, Mr. William Gordon Riddoch, to have dinner with him that evening at 7:00.

"Is Mr. Riddoch here in the hotel now?" Sally asked.

"Yes, Miss Ruth, in his private quarters when here, but he lives in Fountain south several miles from Colorado Springs. May I give him a message?"

"Yes, and please ask Mr. Riddoch if my boyfriend, Mr. Ken Stanley from London in England can join us."

"Yes, Miss Ruth. He is a nice old man and I'm sure he will be okay with the idea. I'll just tell him to expect both you and Mr. Stanley in the dining room at seven."

On time, Ken and Sally entered the large ornately furnished dining room with its many tables and all set with English porcelain bone china and sterling silver dining ware along with folded napkins neatly placed just under the top of each dinner plate. Each table was decorated with floral settings of Colorado's white and lavender Rocky Mountain columbines [which became the State flower in 1899]. A maitre'd expecting their arrival ushered them to the table beside a large picture window in a back corner of the room.

There, Mr. Riddoch arose to greet them cordially. He stood tall, slim and gray-haired and his commanding presence gave him an air of authority of all doings in construction of the hotel even if one knew nothing about him personally. He quickly turned out to be cordial, likable, and well respected.

"I'm Mr. Riddoch." He said to introduce himself. "Welcome to this hotel and you especially Miss Ruth as the new concierge. General Palmer of the Antlers spoke highly of you."

"And of you too, Mr. Riddoch."

"I understand Mr. Stanley that you are from London."

"Yes sir."

"I've been there myself. It's quite a large city with all of its marble palaces, plazas, statues, parks, gardens and zoos. I especially liked the Serpentine Lake in Hyde Park and the Kew Gardens with its greenhouses of tropical plants. A favorite place of mine near the gardens was the Maids of Honour Tearoom. The daily high tea served there with pastries and quiches is, was, excellent to my experience."

"I much agree with that. I visit the tearoom often, but you didn't mention museums, the one where I work...the British Museum of Natural History...which is one of the world's largest with its tens of thousands of butterfly and moth specimens. That's why I'm here...to collect for them more of your so-named Rocky Mountain Apollos."

"What for, may I ask."

"My employer is Mr. Edward Doubleday who in 1874 described the species *Parnassius smintheus* found here in the Rockies and who asked me to collect more for him for additional needed studies of their morphology." Ken grinned with a look at Sally who looked down at her hands when fully expecting to hear the answer already known to her.

"It's been learned, Mr. Riddoch, that among Apollo butterflies the best way to separate closely related species is by…well…taking close looks at the differences in the genitalia of Apollo females. Fifteen years ago Mr. Doubleday didn't then know to look at such to distinguish between species, though now he does and wants more to further support his original description and naming of *P. smintheus* as a valid taxon."

"Oh, I see! I'm sorry now that I asked such a question in front of Miss Ruth, but I guess looking at what you're talking about *would* be of interest to men interested in butterfly taxonomy….and morphology." Mr. Riddoch smiled in the saying. Ken grinned with a look at Sally blushing a bit while still looking down at her hands folded in her lap.

"If you're interested, Mr. Stanley, I think I may know something around here about where to find Apollos, that is if we're talking about the same butterflies. The ones I see are mostly white in color with wide variations in the patterns of their black and red wing spots. Is that true?"

"Yes sir, Mr. Riddoch." Ken exclaimed excited. "Have you seen them recently…maybe in the last day or two?"

"Yes, though not close around here…I guess…because the valley floor is overgrazed each year by cattle and horses and there may not be enough wildflowers for butterflies. But each year it seems between about now and the end of August we see them higher-up in meadows where no livestock graze. Some were seen just yesterday I was told when one of my employees collected the columbines decorating the tables."

"Where was that?" Ken asked excitedly.

"Up a short distance along Crystal Creek."

"Of course! Mr. Riddoch. It's up higher where no livestock graze. We find that true in England where once pristine meadows down in valleys have become hay fields and grass pastures.

"Mr. Riddoch, can we get up along the creek on horses?"

"Not in close but out away. The only way in close is to scramble afoot up over large boulders and steep canyon sides which you can't do on horses or even to get them across the creek from one side to the other. I suggest that you work your way up through the trees on the west side of Mount Esther and now especially since many of the timber trees have been felled for construction lumber and railroad ties. Just tether your horses anywhere along the way up and walk over to the creek. But while you should have no problems with bears watch for them. This is cub season and if you see a mama sow with little ones just go another direction." Mr. Riddoch chuckled. "Remember to her ursine way of thinking, you are on her turf and mother bears don't like trespassers and especially if she feels her cubs are in danger.

"Also as a warning, don't try to go up Catamount Creek on the west side of Mount Rebecca. It's just too hard to get up and down easily. And another thing, keep in mind that there remain in the mountains some, though not many, of the wilder of the Utes who hide out to escape life on reservations and be denied their own culture and religion. They chose not to conform to Euro-American behavioral expectations as taught in Christianity. They have their own Gods and mores often strange to Americans to understand and despite the teachings of Padres and missionaries to 'love thy neighbor as thyself' and 'thou shall not kill,' there remains among ancestral tribes little to no sympathy to forgive and to forget and have no compulsions against murder. To kill an enemy earns a warrior a feather for his bonnet, and to someday be a great chief with a bonnet full of them."

• • • •

By mid-morning of the next day with promises of a pleasant start on an exciting new venture, Ken and Sally saddled up their horses, Prince, gentle to ride, and a hotel stable horse equally gentle being a perk to Sally's new job. Packed in respective saddle bags were the needs of each anticipated for the day, and yet to know the need made at Ken's request, a collection of Sally's hatpins of various colors and a fabric sewing tape measure. Just in case for whatever need Ken carried his Winchester rifle in a saddle holster and his butterfly net tied across the pommel of his saddle. Behind the cantel Ken carried the canvas tarp in case of an afternoon rain. Sally made sandwiches for lunch carried in one saddlebag and in another a handbag of personal items that no girl can ever be without to go just about anywhere. Curious men always wonder about the mysteries inside a girl's handbag though seldom daring to ask about, or to see.

By time of the mid-morning start the day was already warm enough to generate the first of the usual to happen everyday summer thermals that begin swaying the tops of trees. Here and there from off the ground whirlwinds, or dust devils as commonly called, suck up the fluff-ball seeds of summer dandelions and lifted aloft, as well as gossamer spiderlings as tiny balloonists dangling on the ends of long strands of silk spun from their spinnerets.

Sally always had fun with thermals when walking or running into the middle of them and while holding down her dress with one hand so that any boys about couldn't see under, and to hold down her bonnet with the other. Since when a young girl Sally imagined that the billowing cotton-ball tops of cumulous clouds spawned by thermals, to change continuously into the fanciful shapes and figures of animals, people, and the castles pictured in her fairy book stories. A wake of turkey vultures circled high overhead in one thermal and a pair of red-tailed hawks in another.

On the creek side of Mount Esther Ken and Sally worked their way up through the many pines and firs still remaining from logging and in with woodland oaks, elms, aspens and maples. Here and there meadows grew in full bloom, some big some small, and in their pristine nature being where no livestock graze. They were resplendent in the varied colors and hues of blue Lupines and Bellflowers, lavender and white Columbines, Scarlet Paint Brushes, yellow Buttercups, purple Winecups and Thistles. And, yes, in scree areas, patches of red and yellow *Sedum lanceolatum* Stonecrops being the preferred food plant for Rocky Mountain Apollo caterpillars and, finally, the adults themselves, several of them flitting about, their very first to see. Near to one spot at the edge of the meadow, there stood a large Ponderosa pine (**Fig. 11**). "Can we stop here?"

Sally asked. "Beneath is a shady place nice to rest...and besides, it's lunchtime."

The large Ponderosa pine was immediately liked by Ken to be their home base for butterfly studies. In addition to Apollos, Ken took note of the many white and sulphur butterflies of several species flitting about and in with them a variety of swallowtails, fritillaries, skippers, metalmarks, hairstreaks and little blues. Ken knew very well of such butterfly groupings since they also occur in England though there being of different taxons.

The Ponderosa was indeed a nice shady place to rest, and the meadow about seemed to be a gold mine of stuff to study. Even more to their good choice for a home base when later seen, there flowed nearby on Crystal Creek a lovely waterfall down over huge boulders (**Front Cover**) and below a knee-deep pond of snow water melt from off Pike's Peak.

For the fun of it, Sally wrapped her arms around the Ponderosa's huge trunk taking a full arm's length to reach around, and while holding the pose Ken studied her lovely face and, now, standing at their closest not help but notice the intoxicating redolence of Sally's rosewater perfume and it likely being applied with an extra drop or two behind each ear for its purpose. In addition, the tree itself had a delightful vanilla-like fragrance emanating from its bark.

Ken spread out his canvas tarp on which to sit and Sally her sack of sandwiches and cookies along with a container of pink lemonade. Sally removed her bonnet and fluffed out her curly hair. "If we're going to make this Ponderosa home base can we think of a name for it?" She asked.

"We'll have to think on it." He thoughtfully replied.

It had been a good two hours if not a little longer in riding horseback to get to where located and both now leaned back against the Ponderosa for a needed rest and doing little to nothing except just looking around and listening. While all else was quiet, the singing of birds was pleasing to hear with variable songs and warbles. Somewhere near the cooing of Band-tailed Pigeons was heard, and maybe Mourning Doves. The chirps and chips of some kinds of sparrows and finches were heard and seen about out among the meadow plants.

"What kinds are they?" Sally asked.

"I don't know for sure, but wherever I see such as those and don't know their names, I refer to them as LGBs."

"What are those, pray tell?"

"Little Gray Birds," he laughed.

But, by far, the best to hear of any of the singing was that of a male American Mockingbird being somewhere near with its melodious versatilities of songs that at times went on and on for twenty seconds at a time and repeated again and again before switching to the imitations of other birds.

"Ken, do you know that mocking birds also sing at night and sometimes as long as an hour?"

"I didn't know. Why do you think?"

"I don't know either, but they are beautiful to hear when long after dark. I like to drop off to sleep listening. Maybe their singing is sort of like a lullaby…maybe!"

"We have in England a bird called a Nightingale which almost always sings only at night with its own versatilities from throaty chuckles to whistles, and to the purest of treble-like trills, and when heard in the stills of nights are the most beautiful of all birds to hear. Beethoven so loved to hear them he immortalized the flute-like sounds of Nightingales in the Pastoral of his Symphony Number Six. And poet John Milton said of them to warble their sweet notes at night when all in the woods are still, for it is then they tune sweetest their love-labored songs that dost fill the hearts of lovers.

"Furthermore, I think that if there was ever an argument over which bird was heard and the best that sang, an American Mockingbird or an English Nightingale, I think I would go with what Shakespeare once wrote in his Romeo and Juliet about which bird sang, a Nightingale or a Skylark. 'Believe me, my love,' Romeo said. 'It is the Nightingale.'

"One has to know that writers of fiction like Shakespeare are masters in the uses of suggestive metaphors to spice up their stories. He didn't want to outright say that Romeo and Juliet were doing anything improper, which they were," Ken laughed, "but strongly implied it. Remember that Romeo had climbed up Juliet's balcony to be alone with her, but for what reason if need be to ask. Did they spend the night beneath bedsheets? Likely! Moreover, that they heard Nightingales sing is strongly suggestive in the night, and if also hearing Skylarks that like roosters announce the dawn, it was time for Romeo to leave before being found in bed with Juliet. And who knows since Shakespeare didn't say, but likely before climbing out of bed and back down over the balcony the two took time enough for a finale embrace and the ecstasy of another trip to Heaven though likely hurried in the doing."

"Oh hush!" Sally retorted, but Ken continued.

"Writers of poetry and prose use suggestive metaphors to tell their stories and of which uncertain meanings of words are the features of them requiring reader imagination as to what characters are saying or doing when not knowing for certainty what the writer is meaning. Moreover, prudish women like old-maids and those of the cloth who claim to blush when reading sexually stimulating stories are actually thirsting-for the sexual arousal from them as much as men."

"Oh!"

"Read *Fanny Hill* someday…if you haven't already and can find a copy concerning the ribald escapades of an English girl of pleasure, and with chapter by chapter being so full of titillating dalliances that it became the most banned book in history in both England and this country. I suspect that girls who avidly read *Fanny Hill* do so behind closed doors and when not long into the story self-gratify impulsive urges."

"And behind *locked* doors…I'm just guessing."

"I rather think you must have found and read a copy."

"Never mind!"

• • • •

The two sat looking out over the meadow before them trying to count the number of Apollos flying. There seemed at any one time to be as many as eight or ten. "Those are likely mostly males," Ken said, "since it's in the nature of them to… well like the males of any species…spread their genes around and be in continual search of females. And all the while the ladies just sit and sip nectar and perfume the air with clouds of their potent sex pheromones to lure in sex-starved males to… well…you know for what they want."

"I know all about the birds and the bees kinds of stuff. When my sister and I reached and crossed our thresholds of womanhood and began using perfumes, powders, lipsticks, and wearing bustles with ribbons and bows…and lace-trimmed under things I might add…we had motherly lectures about things not to do until married. Well you likely know what she talked to us about."

"I got the same kinds of lecturers when I started shaving and keeping my hair combed, and cologne and all, and it's certainly true of male butterflies to prowl around to *cherchez pour la femmes*, and most often looking for those which have just emerged from their cocoons and even before their wings are dry. It's what's commonly called robbing the cradle." Ken grinned. "I guess that's certainly true since butterfly females never live to be teenagers. Ha!

"One time in England I found the cocoon of an Emperor moth, a large Saturnid silk moth, and placed it in my shirt pocket to carry it home. I had a terrarium there to keep such things alive and I didn't know at the moment it was a female about ready to emerge. But soon thereafter, male Emperors began flying around and alighting on my shirt in search for the virgin treasure inside my shirt pocket. To them…the cradle robbers…she already smelled like a young virgin moth should, and much to my chagrin did what all emerging moths of both sexes do."

"What?"

"Yuck! She excreted all of what was stored up inside her while pupating. What a mess! But aside from that, it's interesting to know that Saturnid moths don't have a proboscis or mouth parts of any kind, so, they can't eat and can survive for only about a week on body fat stored up while caterpillars. Their only purpose in life is to produce fertile eggs for the species to survive and then die soon after. Their job is done. Their eggs are laid on host plants but never see them hatch or get to see their little offspring take their first steps...er crawls." Sally wiped away a make-believe tear though admitted to it being a sad kind of story.

While sitting in the shade of the Ponderosa pine and when watching all going on out in the meadow, numerous species of butterflies and other insects as honey and bumble bees, and dragonflies and such, came in close including Apollos and, fortuitously, close enough to be a witness to the X-rated doings in what's considered the shocking sex habits of butterflies. A female Apollo being little more than an hour old or so alit on a thistle to feed with her long proboscis, first on one flower then others...and spew out sex pheromones. Then what happened was a case of butterfly assault.

Apollo males normally emerge before the females and early-on will patrol for females sometimes at great distances from one meadow to another. It's been so said that males of a species have poor visual discrimination and will investigate all of their genetic Order in general size and color, flying or sitting. While looking for females of their own species they sometimes chase after others of similar appearance.

A patrolling male Apollo on the make suddenly appeared, being lured-in by the sex pheromones of a nearby Apollo

female though confused when seeing close by a Checkered White female (*Pontia occidentalis*) (**Fig. 12**) with spotted and rounded hind wings much like Parnassians. It (he) made a dash for her in error but what happened quickly changed its (his) intent was that the Checkered White closed her wings in an attempt to not be seen, but in failure of that fluttered them in such manner to tell the Apollo that she was not his kind of woman.

It (he) then homed in on the Apollo female but had no intent what so ever of a courtship. With no foreplay involved it was straight to his sole purpose in life. He knocked her to the ground and forced himself into a position for copulation that really couldn't be considered insect rape as she was receptive to his intent and having purposefully lured him in in anticipation of what happened. They stayed attached for nearly an hour when he then deposited a wax-like plug on the tip of her abdomen so that she couldn't mate again. Ken and Sally watched it all happen then when all was over Ken jumped into action and netted the female before she could fly away as he was in need of collecting both virgin and non-virgin specimens. He pinched its thorax.

"Why did you have to do that, the poor thing?"

"I'm sorry but I had to though now she has another purpose in life. I've come here from half way around the world to collect some of these with a sphragis for my employer's studies. But, Sally," he interjected, "had I not come here just for this very reason we would never have met." Such a tender remark resulted in their first kiss, one by Sally though only a peck on the side of his cheek.

"I guess now I'll have to never shave again to save it." Both laughed.

"But look at what I want you to see up close…her chastity belt? Sexy, huh?"

"Not really! But there's no lock on it." Both laughed.

It was already mid-afternoon and time enough yet to enjoy the nearby creek and its water falls before returning to town. The two spent the next hour on Crystal Creek and for a long time when just getting there and while hand in hand watched the water to fall then pool into a shallow pond before flowing on downhill to the next water fall **(Front Cover)**.

"Do you think it would be alright if I wade in it?" Sally asked. "The water looks so cool and nice."

"You don't need permission to wade, and certainly not mine and who's to mind anyway? There is no one else about and I for sure won't care, believe me." Ken grinned.

"Then I'll do it if you won't mind seeing me barefooted."

"Are you kidding? Women's feet are wondrous things for men to see and admire when ballerinas can do a *pas de deux* on tiptoes and when any woman of every temperament can stomp about and kick buckets and shins if so moved. I suppose the world must be full of men who enjoy the sights of women's feet with delicate toes and well-turned ankles, and to some men a woman's foot and toes are fetishes."

"Oh hush with such dumb things to say."

"Well, it's true! In case you didn't know there are the so-called foot men of the world who enjoy sights of pretty feet. The medical field must be full of podiatrists who enjoy their profession and the things they do with feet, and there must be men in shops who are always happy to try shoes on women.

If you don't know of it there are artists who are masters at painting pretty feet, and did you know that some models pose only for feet because theirs are so pretty."

Ken sat on the pond bank and leaned back on his elbows to watch Sally sit and slowly remove her shoes and socks, then stand to swish a foot through the water.

"It's cold!" She gasped. But then without hesitation though with a bit of concern of what she showed, lifted the hems of her dress, petticoat, and her ankle length pantalets decorated with little ribbons and bows up to her knees and step calf-deep into the water.

"Oh my!" Ken exclaimed. "You have lovely knees. I'm glad you wanted to wade or I would probably have never seen them."

"For heaven's sake! Haven't you ever seen a girl's knees before mine?"

"Yes, but not yours, and certainly none prettier, except one time I did see knees like yours on a canary." Ken lay back laughing when seeing the shocked expression on Sally's face to hear such said.

"That wasn't a very nice thing to say." Sally fussed.

"I was just joking." He laughed.

"Well, thank you for saying so…but mine are just plain ole everyday ordinary knees like everyone else's. They don't look anything special to me."

"I'll argue with you on that. You have lovely knees…and your calves aren't bad either, not one bit."

"Oh hush, and anyway there is no one else around to see them…only you."

"Lucky me!" He thought to himself.

There was then a long pause in the inane banter going back and forth and all in fun. Ken watched Sally swish about

65

in the water and in places knee deep and when holding up her dress and the rest to a bit above her knees.

"Ken, would you come in and wade with me? The water is so nice." She said, to then with a devilish grin, kick water in his direction.

"Be careful there or you might get me wet…and believe me you won't want to do that or I might get as mad as a wet hen if you splash me."

"I think you must mean as mad as a wet rooster don't you, or are you saying something quirky about yourself?" Sally grinned and in playful response kicked water again but this time splashing him with several drops.

"Okay you little imp! You've had sufficient warning."

While Ken sat mumbling to himself about things that surely wouldn't be nice for Sally to hear, he slowly and methodically one by one removed his shoes and socks and set each pair aside preparatory to wading in after her. Then, ever so slowly one by one Ken rolled up his pant legs to knee level. The slowness of it all was fully intended to add suspense to what he would likely do, and all along with a glower in pretense. Sally stepped back a little deeper with the hems of her dress and the rest pulled up a little higher. Ken, then, with even more of a pretense glower and a frown across his brow, slowly rolled up the sleeves on both arms and then stood saying: "I just hope for your sake you know how to swim or at least float."

"Ken don't, please. The water is cold and I'm truly sorry I splashed you. I didn't mean to and I can't swim or float. Can we forget what I did?"

"That's nothing *I'm* going to forget. You meant to kick water on me."

Now Ken had no intent to get Sally all wet…to dunk her…only to make her think so, and besides there was no towel to dry her with or a change of clothes. Contrary to what Sally anticipated, Ken picked her up into his arms and hugged her close reveling in the firmness of her bosom buried hard into his chest, the sensual feelings of the undersides of her bare limbs dangling over his bare arms, and the sides of their faces pressed hard together. Sally, though, still a bit anxious, asked: "What are you going to do?"

"Just this!" Ken replied. Then much to both their pleasure turned his face into hers, first with a tantalizing kiss to the middle of her forehead, then the tip of her nose and across both eyes now closed in the pleasure of it all, and then over the side of her face to an ear then down to the tip of her chin and at last a long-wanted long-lasting kiss on Sally's, maybe for all he knew, never before kissed lips. She didn't object and kissed back with an ardor equal to his.

"You know," Sally admitted when back out of the water, back on her feet, and back into her shoes. "I knew all along you weren't going to dunk me."

"I kind of thought all along you knew I wasn't going to dunk you." Both laughed then kissed again although this time with Sally up on her toes.

• • • •

The next morning early for a mid-morning arrival at their Ponderosa pine home base, both saddled up again and this time with Sally's five sets of multicolored hat pins and the thirty-six inch fabric tape measure that had been requested. Ken packed more of his gear including a writing tablet; a kit of assorted pencils and crayons; a twenty-foot tape measure of his own, and more puzzling to Sally, a bottle of India ink and a finger nail paint brush. What the devil for?

On the way up Mount Esther paralleling Crystal Creek, Ken collected more Apollos of which some females had chastity belts though others not as not all were expected to have them since when laying eggs the sphragis plugs are rid of. At the Ponderosa pine they unsaddled their horses for the next hours of work and tethered them to graze in an area rich in montane grasses such as Blue Gramma, Mountain Muly and Arizona Fescue. A bit further uphill from the Ponderosa the two lucked upon a talus slope with a scattering of *Sedum lanceolatum* Stonecrops already in full bloom for the season and being the preferred food for Apollo caterpillars. Of additional importance, the well-exposed sun-lit wind-swept slope was one of the first areas in full sun each spring to be free of winter snow. There, Apollo pupae emerge earlier than those in areas with less sun exposure and lingering snow.

[Rocky Mountain Apollos prefer to inhabit and breed on sites where there are rocks on which both caterpillars and adults can bask and soak up the sun. The higher the elevation in which they live, the bodies of adults tend to be darker for additional warming. On colder days, Caterpillars already black for the purpose also leave their food plants for thermo-regulation on sun-bathed rocks.]

Ken retrieved from a saddle bag the twenty foot tape measure of his own and with Sally's help selected the best clumping of Stonecrops to be delignated as a study transect. Together they erected a rock cairn to mark corner number one of a twenty foot square. Twenty feet over, they erected another cairn for corner number two, then up another twenty feet to corner three and over again to corner number four marking out a four hundred square foot four-cornered square. Within, they mapped and numbered all locations of some thirty stonecrops and, hopefully to find Apollo caterpillars already of fourth or fifth instar age, and already sporting their two mid-dorsal rows of yellow hairy tubercles (**Fig. 13**).

[An instar is a development stage of insects between molts until sexual maturity is reached and being when butterfly caterpillars pupate. The numbers of instars vary among insects. The larvae of Apollo butterflies grow through five instar ages then pupate to turn into adults. Caterpillars must shed their exoskeletons in order to grow into the next instar age and are almost always at a larger size and differences between them being altered body proportions and structures and such. What then develops in the later Apollo instar age, and being kin to Swallowtails of which all their caterpillars have is an osmeterium, an organ just behind the head that when extruded exude a foul smell to fend off predators.]

One by one when down on their hands and knees the two searched each Stonecrop plant even for the smallest of Apollo caterpillars when as first instars are no longer than a grain of rice. Such searches were not easy and being best described as tedious. Plants one and two of Sally's search were for naught but then "Bingo" Sally cried out when she discovered beneath a succulent leaf the first caterpillar and this one large enough at about one inch in length and be already a fourth instar larva.

"Quick, Ken. Come look" who did, and both watched the little fellow feeding and seemingly not bothered being watched. But then it stopped suddenly and began shaking violently, being an effort to scare off predators when Ken tried to measure its length and touched it hard enough.

"Oh phew!" Sally complained when like a jump up out of a jack-in-the-box the caterpillar extruded its stinky foul smelling osmeterium.

"I guess I should have warned you." Ken laughed. "All Parnassian and Swallowtail caterpillars have them to repulse predators, but aside from that you get a gold medal for finding the first one."

"Whoopee! Good for me."

"Now give me one of your hatpins."

"What color?"

"Well, what have you got?"

"I've got two each of five different colors…black, red, blue, green and yellow. Which color do you want?"

"You choose. They're your hatpins."

"I'll go with black since our little fellow here is black. What are you going to do with it?"

"Stick it into our little friend to flag it?"

"Oh no you won't! Not with one of my hatpins." Sally retorted.

"No Silly! Into the Stonecrop it's feeding on. We'll want to come back tomorrow to find this same plant to see if the caterpillar is still feeding on it."

"Oh! But how are you going to know if it's the same caterpillar? Are you going to ask it?" Sally joked.

"No, Nitwit. Like this." Ken grinned in the saying, then removed from a shoulder bag a bottle of black India ink and with a tiny finger nail kind of brush and being very careful about it to not make the caterpillar shake again…gingerly applied a dab of black ink just back of its head and atop the first left-side mid dorsal yellow tubercle (**Fig. 13**)."

"Now you see it, now you don't." Ken gave as an explanation. "You be note keeper and name this plant as Black One and this caterpillar the same name, but meaning that the first yellow tubercle on its left side being number one is painted black. We'll recognize him again and again over the next few days wherever seen and to keep track of where he's going."

"Hey! That's a lot better than a red-hot cattle brand." Sally joked.

Not long after flagging and marking the Stonecrop and its one caterpillar, and when further looking down on their hands and knees, fifteen more caterpillars were found over the next hour that were at least an inch to an inch and a quarter in length to suggest that all were fourth and fifth instars, though three weren't found on plants but basking on nearby rocks. Another seen was crawling between two food plants and most plants showed some measure of being chewed upon. That no plants were completely eaten further suggested that the caterpillars often moved from one food plant to another nearby.

"Why don't they just stay put on one plant until all leaves are eaten?"

"I don't know as it's not uncommon for caterpillars of other species to eat all leaves on a plant before searching for another and that may be the case when females of other species lay their eggs in clusters. Numerous caterpillars hatching on a single plant will quickly eat all of its leaves and have need to then find other plants. That too suggests here that female Apollos lay no more than one egg at a time. But Hey! It's lunchtime."

[In truth, female Rocky Mountain Apollos lay only one egg at a time and not always directly on a Sedum Stonecrop host plant but out from it on sticks and stones though close enough so that just hatched caterpillars can find favored food plants attracted to by their scent.]

The two spent the next hour relaxing beneath the home base Ponderosa and enjoying the sack lunches made for them at the hotel with peanut butter and jelly sandwiches along with pickles and sugar cookies, as well as a container of pink lemonade. Sally brought peppermint sticks.

The forty-eight degree temperature early that morning was now a pleasurable sixty-five. The two shed their coats and positioned themselves to watch all going on out across the meadow in front of them full of wildflowers resplendent of all colors and hues. Ken sat with his back to the Ponderosa and with his arms around Sally backed up against him. For about the next quarter-hour not a word was said, as just sitting close and enjoying their solitude and togetherness was pleasurable enough other than to also watch more and more butterflies of a good number of species.

"What are you seeing?" Sally asked that finally broke the solitude.

"Look over on that thistle." Ken pointed. "What do *you* see?" (**Dedication Picture**).

"If you're talking about the butterfly on it, I don't know what kind."

"It's a Painted Lady common in both England and here in the Americas described way back in the mid-1700s by a Swedish scientist named Carl Linnaeus who was a botanist and entomologist. He described hundreds of flowers and butterflies and dreamed up what's known today as the binomial system of nomenclature in which all plants and animals are given both a genus and a species name. Most names are based on Latin or Greek. The Rocky Mountain Apollos we're studying are known as *Parnassius smintheus* as you've heard spoken of and the name, you claimed, being all Greek to you." Ken chuckled. "In case you didn't know, you and I as humans are given the Latin name *Homo sapiens.*"

"I'm glad to know you, *Homo*," Sally laughed, "though for some reason that doesn't sound very nice."

"Never mind about what it implies. Our binomial in Latin means 'wise human.'"

"I'll buy that!"

"Now, if I can get it to fly, I want you to see what a wise Painted Lady will do to escape a bird predator." Ken threw a stone at the thistle which made it fly.

"Hey!" Sally exclaimed. "That's crazy."

"It's believed the screwy kinds of turns like that they make are reflex actions to sudden scares, being an instinctive way to confuse and escape bird predators. The stone scared it to fly that way. And another strange flight habit of Painted Ladies is that when migrating north for the summer they fly slowly along the entire way to feed and rest here and there, but when migrating south for the winter no one sees them…not in these parts anyway. People down in Mexico and Central America see them, so it's assumed they had flown non-stop at high altitudes all the way down there."

Nothing more was said for another several minutes while watching all going on, when a sudden cool breeze blew in from behind them. Rain clouds back to the west were forming and getting dark, common to happen in mountains in summers.

"I don't see any lightening or hear any thunder!" Sally observed.

"Rain showers don't always have them, not like the storm we sat through down on the Front Range. I'll get the tarp. I think we're going to need it. Henry Wadsworth Longfellow once said that the best thing one can do when it's raining is to just let it rain."

"I'm okay with that...here with you...but do you know what I like best about rain?" Sally asked.

"No. Tell me."

"When I hear rain on the roof at bedtime, it's sort of like a lullaby, and if it's still raining when I awaken I just want to turn over and go back to sleep."

What then followed wasn't hard to describe as to what kind of rain happened. A drizzle is a slow and a long lasting rain that didn't happen. A rain shower, and especially one in summer time when moisture-laden air rises as thermals to cool, then to precipitate is short lasting. That's what did happen. A rain cloud was just passing over ever on the move eastward and all along giving Mother Earth and all living things a good drink of cool fresh rain water. The two sat snug and cozy beneath the tarp listening to the rain, but only for a minute or two before abating and stopping. What then enjoyed was the after-smell of a fresh rain emanating from everything wet.

"Did you hear it too?" Sally asked.

"I heard the rain. What else was I supposed to hear?"

"I don't know for sure, but it seemed to me anyway that during the rain this old Ponderosa was whispering something. It sounded sort of like...well...a 'thank you,' maybe for the rain."

"I suppose that could be true. The tree was thirsty and thanked Mother Nature for the rain, but maybe it was only the wind through the tree you heard."

"Maybe, but remember we had wondered about a name for this old tree. What about 'The Whispering Tree?'"

Soon both were back to the transect where four more Stonecrops were flagged with two red colored hatpins as Red One and Red Two and two yellow colored hatpins as Yellow One and Yellow Two. Ken inked another four caterpillars by blacking out their respective next-in-line left-side tubercles, now numbering five and six since the first one of the day before. All measured to between one and an eighth to one and a quarter inch in length to suggest they were already fifth instar caterpillars and soon to pupate. By mid-afternoon when all the work was done it was time to wade again with all the fun of it ending up with more kicking of water back and forth.

By mid-morning of the next day, both were back to the Whispering Tree home base and ready again to flag more Stonecrops and ink-mark caterpillars. But there was now a perplexing problem. It wasn't to relocate the Stonecrops as their locations were well mapped and easy to find by their colorful hatpin flags. The problem was that the marked caterpillars were nowhere found as much as looked for.

[Rocky Mountain Apollo caterpillars will feed upon more than one Stonecrop and at times no longer than an hour before moving to another. Only three or four leaves may be fed upon at any one time but can be easily detected by the visible chew scars on them. The next available plant could be only inches away or up to many and which are likely found by scent. Moreover, feeding time can be short-lived. A late instar caterpillar can eat a leaf in about three minutes to then move to another plant. It may be as in other plants that Sedum Stonecrops have self-defense methods to sense being fed upon and make themselves less palatable with chemical repellants which would explain why within minutes a caterpillar is discouraged to feed any longer on an attacked plant and will go find another.]

Back down on their hands and knees the two searched diligently for the missing inked caterpillars and sure enough another three were found, identified by which of their tubercles were marked. Of interest, two were found basking on nearby rocks which supported belief that the caterpillars will spend as much or more time off their food plants than on them. Their black color further helps them to warm faster on cold mornings. And, too, the dark bodies of adults will do the same thing and referred to as thermal regulation. One caterpillar that couldn't be found supported the opinion that it had already pupated somewhere beneath leaf litter and loose soil and would remain there until the next spring and only after the snow melts, living up to its "snow butterfly of the mountains" moniker.

Sally used her sewing tape to measure the distances traveled by the two caterpillars basking in the sun and the three found on other plants. "Good going! Right on!" Ken exclaimed to know what Sally found. The two "sun bathers" found suitable rocks within three feet warm enough on which to bask, and the three found on other plants had moved no more than two feet to find them.

"Great!" Ken exclaimed again and kissed Sally atop her forehead for the finding. Sally grinned by the affectionate compliment and being careful to not wipe it away. Ken sat for a few minutes to record the findings in his notebook.

It again was time for lunch beneath the Ponderosa after which the remainder of the afternoon was spent collecting butterflies of which a wide variety were now flitting about out in the meadow including more Apollos. Sally collected some by stealth approaches to net those feeding or resting. Some were chased on the run over sticks and stones and through thistles. Sally's bonnet tied tightly beneath her chin kept both hands free; one to hold and swing the net and the other to lift the hems of her dress and petticoat to keep from tripping when on the run. Ken, once, heard Sally mutter "damn it" when she did stumble, and "dang it" when a thorn bush snagged and tore her dress. Ken grinned each time. One time when upset by missing a catch Sally stood with her hands upon her hips and a frown across her furrowed brow. Sally was just fun to watch when collecting butterflies.

This day in a stealth approach to net an Apollo Sally saw feeding on a flower but stopped suddenly when seeing it close and called out: "Ken...quick...come look...there's two of them doing it! One is feeding on a flower while the other is...well... just hanging on (**Fig. 14**) doing what it's doing tail to tail like that, and why not in missionary style?"

"Or in doggy style." Ken replied and laughed when he too looked. "The male is holding onto her...her lady part...with his claspers," Ken explained, "but either up-or-down or back-to-back or tail-to-tail describes what's happening depending upon one's point of view." Ken laughed. "He will hang on like that for at least an hour to keep another male from horning in on his one call in life which is to fertilize a female's eggs."

"Will he leave her with a chastity belt?" Sally asked with a smile, having been told of such and having read titillating tales about medieval knights and their "locked-up" ladies and when being away as long as on Crusades? Heaven forbid!

By mid-morning of the next day a search for the six inked caterpillars proved fruitless, surmised to have pupated already. Ken however felt they had learned enough just from the six studied. Sally recovered her hatpins; Ken flattened the four cairns that marked the transect corners; then it was back by both to collect more butterflies in the meadow that stretched out before their Whispering Tree home base.

By then it was lunchtime and with the weather much warmer the meadow that stretched out before them was alive with butterflies. It was a glorious day. Both shed their coats and after lunch with little further said of one thing or another, relaxed half-asleep with Sally's head upon Ken's shoulder and an arm across his chest. Then when up and about, more butterflies were collected followed by another much-fun knee deep wade in Crystal Creek with more kicks of water back and forth.

The next morning being a Saturday, May 19, 1889, was leisurely spent exploring the nooks and crannies of Green Mountain Falls though yet having only a few streets, dwellings and businesses. Here and there in-close on the 160 acre original tract, first used as a meadow for livestock, the budding new town already had a church, school, post office and a small number of homes and businesses. The coming of the Colorado Midland Railway three years earlier with a Depot was a boon to the town. The square dance planned that evening in the new hotel's ballroom was in part to commemorate the hotel's grand opening being the first for the community then spoken of only as The Hotel then later The Green Mountain Falls Hotel.

Ken and Sally were eager to attend as dance partners but at the moment inside his tent-cabin rental and to her puzzlement watched him open a bottle of a locally acquired home brewed beer and mixed in with it a cup of rum molasses used for his morning flapjacks. As a final ingredient Ken stirred in more and more brown sugar until all was thickened into a pasty semi-intoxicating alcoholic concoction of rum-scented sorts.

"What are you going to do with *that*?" Sally asked.

"Drink it!" Ken answered, jokingly. "Wanna join me?"

"I'll pass, thank you. Are you really going to drink that... that...whatever it is?"

"It's for *moths* to drink." He explained. "As thick as it is I'll paint it on tree trunks, and moths in the night attracted to its enticing aroma will be found inebriated in it or near about in the morning and being too tipsy to fly." He laughed. "A cloth of some sort spread out below the bait will collect those that fall off. Others will stay put and I'll net those."

"How do you catch them if they can't fly?"

"There are two ways that work. First, though, begin with the moths closest to the ground. If you start with those at the top the net hanging down will disturb those immediately below. Put the rim of the net just below the specimen wanted and touch it. Those that can't fly will drop down into the net. Some won't even flutter in trying to get out."

"But what if they can fly?"

"If it takes off when touched, a quick upward sweep of the net may catch it. If not, watch where it goes. Most inebriated moths won't fly far before alighting again. Some of them as well as tipsy butterflies will be so lethargic they can be coaxed to sit on a finger."

"Can I help?"

"I was hoping you would ask." Ken grinned. "We'll wait until just before the square dance starts to bait a number of tree trunks to keep off the daytime flies and hornets and such, and then check the baits early after sunrise. Otherwise, predators of one kind or another may get them first. You can stay the night here for an early start if you want and sleep on the bed. There are enough chair cushions, bed pillows and extra blankets around for me to sleep on a pallet and when up I'm good at making breakfast flapjacks British style."

"Are they the same as pancakes?"

"Not quite, but better! They are baked and eaten sort of like a brownie, and with molasses on them if wanted."

Sally spent much of the rest of the day at the hotel preparing for her work as concierge. Most positions would require around-the-clock assignments in three eight-hour shifts. Sally's would be from eight in the morning until five in the evening with an hour off for lunch and weekends.

Early that evening the two dined on Sally's homemade vegetable soup, and about an hour before dark painted the intoxicating moth bait brew in areas of about one square foot head-high on the sides of ten nearby tree trunks, and then it being square dance time.

Dressed for the occasion Sally wore a red gingham dress with puffed sleeves, a curved neckline, and with a full skirt in two lengths styled for fast dance step whirls and twirls with skirts flying (**Fig. 15**). Ken wore a long-sleeved shirt with a string bow tie and an open vest common for western attire in square dances.

By seven that evening the hotel was packed with locals and those from neighboring towns and visiting dignitaries invited for the inauguration of Saturday night square dances promised by Mr. F. E. Dow, president of

Green Mountain Falls Town and Improvement Company to be traditional through the year when weather permitted. Mr. W.G. Riddoch, hotel builder, welcomed all. Dow and Riddoch were accompanied by their wives as square dance partners. German Count James M. Pourtales was present and who also received applause in thankful appreciation when just that afternoon swam out into the lake to rescue Mrs. Dow and child when her boat overturned. Count Pourtales then stood to more applause later when he introduced as a dancing partner his beautiful cousin, Countess Berthe de Pourtales who he later married.

Also present for the square dance were George Howard, former rancher of the valley flat and his wife, and Ogden Whitlock who built the first house in the valley and his wife. There was another applause given in the honor of Mr. W. J. Foster, real estate dealer and general manager of the Green Mountain Falls Company and his wife who just a few years earlier bought the valley for the purpose of making it into a summer resort and who named it Green Mountain Falls.

Of the about forty people then permanently living in Green Mountain Falls there were enough dancers to form two squares. The dignitaries formed another three. The hotel employees who participated including Sally and her partner formed two more. In addition, there were enough children to form a square, being eight in all. All others at the dance watched the fun of it all and who if so moved clapped their hands and/or tapped their toes to the music.

A fiddler with his lively bow and a caller hired for the jobs called several square dances but the first one, a favorite and later called twice more went:

> Bow to your partners, then corners all
> Bow to your partners across the hall
> Ladies to the center and back once more

Gents star right in the middle of the floor
Go around the lady, do the figure eight
Back around the gent and don't be late
Chase that rabbit, chase that squirrel
Chase that girl all around the world
Chase that rabbit, chase the raccoon
Chase that boy right around the room
Promenade two and promenade four
Keep that calico off the floor
Now all join hands and circle eight
Now promenade home and bow to your mate
Then do it all again till you have it straight
Bow to your partners, the corners all
Bow to your partners across the hall

The girls and their partners bowed and swung, sashayed forward and sashayed back, do-si-doed and promenaded, then circled and whirled with their curls and skirts flying until they thought they would drop from the all of it (**Fig. 16**). Between square dances the evening wore on with folk dances as "Jim along Josey," "Leather Britches," "Roaring River," and then others as "Old Zip Coon," "Rosin the Bow," "My Wife's Dead," and the ever popular "Turkey in the Straw," "Put Your Little Foot," and the "Two Step." The two never had so much fun and to have lasted through the dances almost exhausted.

• • • •

"Wake up, Sally." Ken said when he nudged her arm early the next morning. Sally awoke with a start and sat up looking around as if for a moment not knowing where she was.

"Oh God Ken! What time is it?"

"It's time to go check on the moth baits. The sun is coming up, and I've already got the coffee brewing."

"What happened?" Sally asked when yawning and while rubbing the sleep out of her eyes.

"As soon as we got back last night late you plopped face down on the bed. That was the last of anything I heard out of you...until just now for us to go check on the moth baits."

"Oh, Ken, I'm so sorry, and thanks for the blanket you must have tossed over me. But last night I was dead on my feet after all the dancing and just crashed when getting back. How did you sleep? How was the pallet?"

"Not too bad really, and you obviously slept well since it took another nudge or two to wake you."

"Well, turn your head for a minute and let me get out of this square dance dress into something else I brought."

"Can I help?"

"*No*, thank you! Just turn your head as I asked."

Both had a breakfast of scrambled eggs, British style flapjacks, and Bourbon Santos coffee that Ken liked strong enough to dissolve nails and float horse shoes, he claimed.

"Well it does taste good, but Bourbon is a funny name for coffee. Isn't that a kind of liquor?"

"Not in this case." Ken laughed. "The name comes from the island of Bourbon in the Indian Ocean from where its seeds were planted in Brazil. It's the best of the Santos varieties grown in the highlands of Sao Paulo. It's claimed that the higher coffee trees grow the richer they are in flavor, and it was from there that the beans are now exported into England in Liverpool and then by train down to London. I grind the beans myself and brought the bag of grounds."

Then, promptly, both went to check on the moth bait results and to happy findings five hawkmoths of three species were seen, one a rarity (**Fig. 17**) being a Pink-spotted Hawkmoth (*Agis cingulata*) more common to the south of Colorado but sometimes found well up into the State. It sat inebriated and when touched flashed its rows of bright-colored pink spots down both sides of its abdomen and best of all the large pink spots on its hind wings.

Two Tobacco Hawkmoths (*Manduca sexta*) were seen (**Fig. 18**) often called tomato hornworms being infamous to farmers and gardeners in eating tomato, potato and

tobacco plants. Much to Sally's amusement and delight it sat

on her index finger and at times flutter its wings so fast to seem only as a blur but it never flew. It had rows of yellow spots.

There were two of the third hawkmoth species (**Fig. 19)** being White-lined Sphinx (*Hyles lineata*) or Hummingbird moths commonly seen flying in the daytime when feeding on flowers much the same as do hummingbirds. They, too, were inebriated and lethargic and dropped into the net and of which one, too, also sat on Sally's index finger much to more of her delight.

Also found on the baits were a number of Underwing moths but difficult to identify as to species because they looked too much alike with the near-to-the same orange and/or red-colored hindwings (**Fig. 20)**. One did fly but being typical of Underwing moths it flew for only a short distance before stopping. Ken netted it.

The only one caught not on a bait that Sally liked most was a large and very pretty bright yellow Io moth (*Automeris io*)

(**Fig. 21)** with large hind-wing eye spots that also scare predators. Quite by chance it was seen on a nearby willow tree and like all silk moths of its family it doesn't have a proboscis or mouth parts of any kind and lives only about a week subsisting on stored-up body fat when as a caterpillar it fed largely only on willows.

Ken couldn't help bypassing the opportunity to tease Sally again about the only silk moth in England, the Emperor (*Saturnia pavonia*) that even while emerging the females of its kind were already filling the air with their clouds of potent sex pheromones and when males from miles around arrived *haste fast* to service the young virgin even before she could fly...and even if she wanted to get away." Ken laughed.

The remainder of the day was a lazy one. The two walked over to and around the lake, and rowed a boat out to sit in under the gazebo. Boys playing in the water were trying to stand of a floating log, but the fun of it was being rolled off and splashing and laughing. Other boaters were out fishing, but a sailor in a little sloop wasn't doing much of anything as the day at the time was windless.

Catawampus from the lake was a tavern and within at a soda fountain Ken and Sally enjoyed the new wild cherry phosphate beverages and while listening to one of the new coin-operated music boxes with a windup crank to hear them play. Afterward, they walked to the Colorado Midland Depot to look for a time at a train idling and then with lots of steam and smoke started up uphill again with steam whistles and clangs of bells to Woodland Park and Divide.

"Let's do it!" Ken suggested. Both checked the next day's train schedules for the uphill grind to Divide getting there at eleven, and to return on another train at four from Cripple Creek and Leadville on its way to Manitou and Colorado Springs through Green Mountain Falls.

They did it! On its way to Divide at the top of the Pass the train stopped in Woodland Park which by mid-morning was busy about town being the business and population center of Teller County although Cripple Creek was the county seat. Most of the people seen were walking or riding in horse-drawn carriages or ox-drawn wagons. The Crest Hotel with fifteen bedrooms was newly built and it being then the only hotel in town.

Though it doesn't always happen according to schedules, the train arrived timely in Divide and when Ken and Sally began walking about and as almost always anywhere now hand-in-hand. Being lunchtime they went into Harkin's Drug Store for a sandwich each and a cherry phosphate drink at the soda fountain. Sally chose the plain cherry drink and Ken one with a wild cherry flavor. Each sipped the other's drink for taste comparisons though it was decided that the wild cherry phosphate was a bit the better. To be polite about it, Ken switched his wild cherry phosphate with Sally's plain cherry. "Thank you," she said with a polite squeeze on his hand.

A block away stood George Sandler's Merchandise Store. "Let's go in and look around." Sally said. "Maybe there's something we can't live without." Ken said. Once in, it became quite obvious that the store smelled airless from a shortage of windows and inadequate ventilation even with the front and back doors propped open. More so were the musty telltale hints of bats in the attic and mice in the store.

Just inside the back door at a roll-top desk with pigeon holes crammed, Mr. Sandler with graying hair and wearing Ben Franklin spectacles sat busy with paperwork. Near to him atop a hay bale a large calico cat that earned her keep as a mouser slept peacefully. Sally scratched behind her ears that awoke the cat with a start to then meow hoarsely and turn over as if to say "Now scratch my tummy, please."

Displayed on shelves all about were bolts of calico, gingham, flannels, wools, linens, toweling, and spools of thread, lace, ribbons and bolts of colored yarns. Still more displayed about were shoes and socks, buttons, beads, hooks and snaps, dishes and flatware, along with cooking utensils such as pots, pans and skillets as well as kettles of all kinds. Feeds and seeds, sacks of flour, oats and cornmeal, and glass containers of spices, crackers, hard cookies, rock candy, licorice and cinnamon and peppermint sticks and all that added to the potpourri of smells in the store, aside from the hints of bats and mice.

To Ken's interest were displays of hand guns and long rifles. For the fun of it, Ken shouldered an 1873 .45-70 caliber Springfield trap-door breech-loading rifle and in pretense took aim, pulled on the trigger, and with an audible "boom" uttered rocked back knowing how rifles kick. Mr. Sandler smiled in seeing and hearing the make believe act.

"Heavens!" Ken remarked to Sally. "There's just about anything a person could ever want is found in here." Mr. Sandler overhearing smiled again, as did Sally looking at intimate things. A bust displaying a new style of brassiere and another of knee length bloomers caught Ken's attention.

While he further looked over the displays of hardware items and such, Sally opened the New York Godey's Lady's Book and made a quick look to see that Ken wasn't watching, then paged through pictures of "unmentionables" such as corsets, night gowns, chemises, bloomers, pantalets, and feminine apparel as aprons, crinolines, fans and purses. Just as she was looking through The Baltimore's Hoffman and McLaughlin Emporium catalogue at the very newest styles of uplifting cup-shaped brassieres, low-cut blouses and wedge-shaped heels Ken walked up and Sally quickly shut the catalogue. Both went back outside sucking on peppermint sticks after buying a bag of them at a penny each, and being the one and only thing in the store they couldn't live without.

By then, it was near to the time of arrival and departure of the Midland back to Green Mountain Falls. Not long in the waiting, they heard off in the far distance the steam whistle of the four o'clock train that soon arrived, and further heard were the hisses of steam from its boilers, valves, compressors and pistons and the shrill sounds of its steam whistle and the clang of its bell while pulling to a stop in the station, all of which created quite a din and caused people to step back out of the bursts of steam released across the platform.

Much to their surprise they heard their names called out. Miss Ruth...Mr. Stanley, and when looking for the source saw climbing down from the cab the same engineer who drove the train the day they arrived in Green Mountain Falls. Cordial greetings were exchanged followed by the engineer's invitation to the two to once again ride in the cab for the short downhill ride to Green Mountain Falls. Again along the way Sally pulled down on the whistle cord at road crossings and when stopping in Woodland Park, and again in The Green Mountain Falls depot. There, too, with Sally's train having the right of track another train going uphill sat idling on a siding waiting for them to pass. Aside from cordial "thank yous" for the offer of another cab ride and, of course, a helping hand to get in and out, Sally gave a peppermint stick each to the engineer and his fireman.

Just before dark that evening the two painted the last of the inebriating molasses-rich rum bait for moths and spent the remainder of the evening to another home-cooked meal to Sally's serving, and late into the night playing card games in the light of a kerosene lantern. Following games of Go Fish, Crazy Eights and Pinochle Ken thought to suggest a game of Strip Poker but then decided against it. Sally was much too good at playing card games.

Early the next morning Sally again awoke with a start when nudged awake to check on the moth baits.

"I could have slept on the pallet and let you have the bed last night." Sally apologized while again yawning and wiping

away the sleep in her eyes, to then cook breakfast while Ken tended to the coffee.

The nighttime catches were especially good with another Hawkmoth species (**Fig. 22**), a One-eyed Sphinx (*Smerinthus cerisyi*) also with large eye spots that scare bird predators.

When with all wings fully closed its hard-to-see bark-like appearance made it look much alike the tree itself. "Look on the lichen patches. What do you see there?" Ken asked.

"What am I supposed to see?"

"A moth…and there are three of them."

"I don't see *one*. How big are they?"

"About half the length of your thumb."

"I still don't see one (**Fig. 23**)."

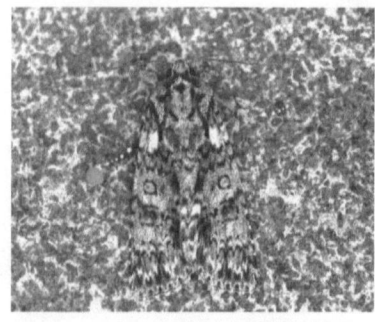

"Watch!" He said. Ken put his net beneath one of the moths resting on a patch of gray-white lichens and when touched dropped down inside with no attempt to fly.

"Okay! Now I see the other two, but how did you know what to look for?"

"I learned in looking for similarly camouflaged moths we have in England…one being the Oak Beauty and another being the Peppered Moth. They too are difficult to spot as their wings blend in so well with the patterns of tree bark and lichens. Even of more interest, the Peppered Moth is one of the best examples of so-called industrial melanism. Over time it came to look dark much like soot in industrial areas but remained light in its original color in forests. An Oxford entomologist once released normal and dark forms in the unpolluted countryside and in polluted cities when the comparisons of predation by birds confirmed that light-colored moths were undetected in the countryside and dark moths in the cities."

"Clever! What's the name of these moths here?"

"Common Gray Moths (*Anavitrinella pampinaria*) (**Fig. 24**) being rather apt in their name, I think, as they *are* gray in color like tree bark and are common where found because they escape bird predation. The name makes sense, and if one thinks Common Grays are good at camouflaging then their caterpillars are the masters of disguise. In the presence of bird predators they stand erect and stiffen their slender bodies in ways that make them look like twigs."

• • • •

The next day was a Wednesday and for the first time plans were made to go all the way to the top of the Crystal Creek waterfalls. There too are rocky pinnacles atop Mount Esther which Ken hoped to collect any of the so-called hill topper butterflies, common for the males of some species to set up territories to patrol for females of their kind and to fight with other males not only over territories but over females.

However, such an effort would take longer than a day, and planned ahead was to take a third horse from the hotel stable for back packing such as a tent, sleeping bags, canvas tarp and such and to have enough food even for a third day of camping if decided. A change or two of clothes, warm coats for nighttime temperatures, and a good supply of matches for campfires as well as Ken's rifle if need be.

After a mid-morning start, a stop was made for lunch beneath the Whispering Pine and to watch more of the amusing to see butterfly shenanigans. Up close the tiniest of the sulphur butterflies, a Dainty Sulphur (*Nathalis iole*), flying low to the ground and feeding on asters suddenly chased after a female of its kind and which seemingly in the way he fluttered his wings was showing off his colors to impress her. Sally smiled while watching the little male do his thing but rejected when the little female flew away.

"I'm sorry little guy." Sally said to it in sympathy and as she wiped away a make-believe tear.

"You're such a softie." Ken said in pretense empathy.

The two rechecked the former transect study area near to the Whispering Pine and found no more of their ink-marked caterpillars as most had likely pupated already. When down on their hands and knees looking for any cocoons under loose leaf litter and shallow soil, they did find three that may have been marked ones, but in other areas of Stonecrop food plants they found another five cocoons.

"These eight will be going back for Mr. Doubleday to see them emerge in his laboratory terraria. Male butterflies are believed to be the first to emerge and the females a day or two later. He'll determine if that is true with Apollos and also have virgin females fresh out of their cocoons for his studies of their...their lady parts." Ken grinned. Sally blushed.

In the steeper places when going uphill it seemed easier on both people and horses to go it afoot, and for Ken and Sally to lead the horses along behind them. But every so often rests of man and animal were good for all and when it gave chances for the three horses to graze a bit and for Ken and Sally to sit awhile. "Oh me!" Both claimed when during rest occasions they sat back against trees.

Still later when nearing the peak of Mount Esther, things began leveling out and the surrounding forest of woodland oaks, elms and aspens grew in with pines, spruces and firs. Moreover, the trees up high were denser in number where none had been logged. There, though, too many had low hanging limbs to sit astride horses. Both, slowly, worked their way afoot up through the trees and understory brush, but when Ken's horse suddenly stopped, snorted and pricked its ears when sensing something amiss. The other two horses did the same and both Ken and Sally knew the meaning of a horse's ears pricked forward and especially so when alerted to a strange sight, sound or alien smell. Both looked in the same direction as the horses though saw nothing.

Maybe the horses had sensed the nearby presence of a bear, or a mountain lion or maybe a pack of wolves, not at all uncommon in the mountains. Ken took the Winchester rifle from its saddle holster in case of sudden need, though after a time and with no little apprehensive suspense, the horses relaxed their ears and began grazing again. Ken put the rifle back into its holster.

At the time however it seemed that nothing could be  wilder than the forest they were now within though not much further uphill a small clearing appeared which in part was capped by a pinnacle of large boulders enticing to climb for an overall view and where far below the Green Mountain Falls valley was plainly seen. For a time Sally stood atop the pinnacle taking in the all of it (**Fig. 25**). Cumulus clouds up high and slowly drifting were promises of a good day of warm weather with no rain, much hoped for when camping out.

"Ken, I'm not sure what I just heard down by the creek but something there ran off fast into the trees. It must have seen me. Do we have deer here?"

"Deer do live in forested areas. Maybe you heard one, though there are no doubt other kinds of animals about. But while it's still early enough I want us to check out the pinnacle for any of the so-called hill topper butterflies and bait them with the rotting banana I brought that you had wondered about. Butterflies often feed on fermenting fruit like black berries and such and even get tipsy."

[Hill-topping habits in butterflies facilitate the meeting of the sexes, especially among certain Skippers, Coppers, Blues, Parnassians and Swallowtails, being those kinds which tend to congregate on hill tops or along rocky ridges higher usually than the surrounding countryside and which may vary in size from a few square yards to many acres. In some cases it could be only a tree stump, a fence post or the top of a big rock or the tip of a twig. Hill-toppers are males that tend to establish breeding territories; defend them from other males; and within patrol for (search for) females of their kind, and which are usually the just-emerged virgins that enter in search for mates. Afterwards, impregnated, they fly off in search for food plants to lay their eggs.]

After a short time of looking, a Black Swallowtail (*Papilio polyxenes*) was seen resting on a thistle maybe tired from hill topping and to Sally's asking, netted it and as usual in team effort Ken pinched its thorax while Sally made the envelope to keep it. Also seen and netted in one sweep Ken caught two Gray Copper males (*Lycaena dione*) spiraling around one another in a fight over disputed breeding territory. Nearby, a pair of little Gray Hairstreaks (*Strymon melinus*) sat in tandem on a flower doing what butterflies do. When off the pinnacle and the sun was beginning to set, Ken pitched the tent barely big enough for two and in between two large boulders providing a protected place for the night.

"You sleep in the tent tonight." Ken suggested to Sally who from the start had wondered somewhat about sleeping arrangements. "It looks like it's going to be clear tonight with no rain and a sky full of stars. I'll sleep outside with the Winchester and tend to the fire just in case wild animals come sniffing around…maybe wolves and bears. Maybe you heard one of them at the creek."

"You're just trying to scare me but with you sleeping out don't forget ghosts, goblins and bad fairies." Both laughed.

Nearby among towering Ponderosa Pines and Douglas Firs there grew a smaller Piñon Pine. Sally knew about the importance of them to Ute Indians, being pine cone nut food high in fats and rich in calories. Moreover, she knew that Piñon firewood burned with a pleasing aromatic aroma.

"Let's get some." Sally suggested. The two gathered an arm load each of broken-off limbs and twigs, and while he lit a fire with it for cooking she prepared a salivary repast in a frying pan and it being a full meal in itself. Sally peeled and sliced four white potatoes, along with a carrot. an onion, and one tomato; a half-cup of canned mushrooms; then sprinkles of shredded Cheddar cheese to top it off, and to all for flavor two tablespoons of Worcestershire sauce along with pinches of salt and pepper. Too, Ken boiled a percolator pot of Bourbon Santos coffee that added a pleasurable aroma to that of the Piñon firewood and cooking meal.

After dinner when sitting around the campfire roasting marshmallows and while contemplating the heavens and constellations, bedtime came. The day had been long and tiring, and Ken's offer of the tent to Sally had answered without her having to ask about who would sleep where. Victorian era propriety, demeanor and decorum, ruled out together but being contrary to mutual suppressed desires.

Ken was up at the break of a new day and while Sally slept he investigated the creek for animal tracts. Suspected as Sally had thought and heard were indeed the cloven foot prints of deer, but a bit surprising to having been so close to the camp in the night were wolf or coyote paw prints, *and* the unquestionable large paw prints of a bear that clearly showed toe and claw marks. Fortunately as it may have happened, the campfire had kept all at bay.

Moreover much to his surprise Ken discovered an old Ute teepee-like wickiup though obviously long unused (**Fig. 26**). He peaked inside.

[In mountainous areas Ute Indians stacked tree limbs together covered with brush or animal hides to form shelters called wickiups. Those still seen like the one pictured were most likely used before the Utes were forced onto Reservations though suggesting that while some later escaped returned to live in them in remote areas and be well hidden to escape eventual recapture.]

Ken returned to tell Sally about his finds and who by then was up stoking the fire in preparation for cooking breakfast and boiling a morning pot of coffee.

"Before doing that I want to show you some things of interest." Along the creek Ken pointed out the hoof prints of deer, and perhaps some of the one she thought she heard run off, and the bear paw prints as well as those that may have been of a wolf or a pack of them.

"It must have been lucky for us having a campfire last night." Sally commented on seeing them.

"Likely. Most wild animals are thought to have fears of fire, but aside from the tracks I want you to see a wickiup."

"Neat!" Sally exclaimed and explained on seeing her first one, and when down on her hands and knees peeking inside. "There's no room in here for more than two, and certainly not big enough to stand up in." Sally commented. "Not long ago," she continued, "there was a meeting at the Antlers about Indian history in Colorado with one topic discussed being about wickiups in which Utes lived in forested areas and in tipis out on the plains. Little ones like these were believed to be only temporary shelters when used by a hunter or two, maybe like this one being near to the creek. Larger family-sized wikiups were lived-in year around. Neat!" Sally said. "Let's crawl in."

Once inside, the room was big enough for two to sit and just large enough to lie down prone that worked in the trying. "Neat" both exclaimed but when looking up and seeing cob webs with spiders they hurried out. "Yuck!" Sally fussed.

Once back to the pinnacle the two enjoyed a mid-morning breakfast of scrambled eggs and this time with pancakes and maple syrup. The day by then had warmed enough for butterflies to be out and about. The two climbed back atop the pinnacle to check on success of the rotting banana bait.

27   28

29   30

Sure enough feeding on it were two Red Admirals (*Vanessa atalanta*) (**Fig. 27**), a Mourning Cloak (*Nymphalis antiope*) (**Fig. 28**), a Hoary Comma (*Polygonia gracilis*) (**Fig. 29**), and interesting to see both together, a Question Mark (*Polygonia interrogationis*) (**Fig. 30**) and when with wings closed displayed their easily identifiable punctuation wing marks. In addition were a number of Yellow Jackets, unidentified beetles, flies of some kind with house fly similarities, and a multitude of tiny Drosophila fruit flies, those with red eyes, and a host of unidentified ants.

"They look like sugar ants to me." Sally commented.

With a slow and cautious approach to not alarm the butterflies engrossed in their feeding, and each with a long proboscis, Ken took a quick swing just above them to catch all five in one sweep and it being his best catch ever with a net. Interesting especially to him were the Red Admirals and Mourning Cloaks being common in both the Americas and in England and both in most of the United States, though in England the Mounting Cloak is known as a Camberwell Beauty having been discovered in the village of Camberwell two miles south of London, A near identical species also named Comma (*Polygonia c-album*) occurs in England.

> [Comma butterflies in general delight in sunshine, and will bask for hours with wings wide spread. They tend to be solitary and have favorite perch points, such as particular twigs or leaves. They may live in an area as small as a few square yards, sipping nectar from flowers, or feeding on rotting fruit or dripping tree sap. Commas are the butterfly experts at disguise. Not only will the caterpillars of some Commas look like bird droppings the adults are well camouflaged with ragged-looking wings to resemble frayed leaves. Adults survive winters by hibernating in such places as tree hollows.]

From their vantage point Ken happened to notice down below a dark colored butterfly flying about the top of the same Piñon Pine of firewood supply. Its flight pattern was not at all unlike the patrolling habit of hill topper males in search for females and in this case being the top of a tree.

"What kind is it?" Sally asked.

"I don't know at the moment…it's too far away to tell." When down and on closer look both were excited to see that it was a Great Purple Hairstreak (*Atlides halesus*) (**Fig. 31**) being the first one seen and a male by its colorations.

"Darn it!" he exclaimed. "It's up too high to catch."

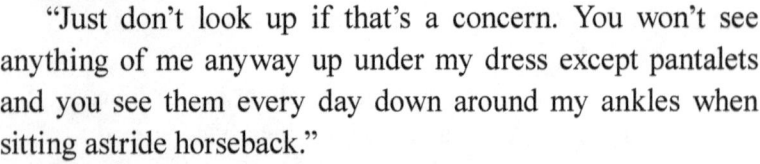

"I've been good for years when climbing trees. Let me catch it. Just hand me the net when I get up."

"But you can't do that in a dress. It's not proper."

"Just don't look up if that's a concern. You won't see anything of me anyway up under my dress except pantalets and you see them every day down around my ankles when sitting astride horseback."

"How about up above your knees when wading?"

"That too…but as I said for your eyes only."

"Well good for me…anytime," Ken laughed, "but you can't risk falling and breaking an arm or a leg just before starting work soon at the hotel. I can climb the tree myself." The effort worked and when up high enough and when close enough on a patrol flight Ken netted the Hairstreak.

"Jolly good show!" Sally called up in pretense English English when seeing the catch.

"Right on!" Ken replied similarly, and quickly pinched its thorax to stop its fluttering. It was in perfect condition with all four tails, and a specimen to be prized when taken back to the British Museum. In a joint effort, Sally folded a glassine envelope for it and helped pack it carefully in the cigar box kind of a treasure chest already full of valuables.

Yet that day there was still another prize to add when an Arizona Sister (*Adelpha eulalia*) (**Fig. 32**) was seen feeding on sap seeping out of an oak tree branch (or limb) and being much alike *Parnassius smintheus* it was a species named by Ken's boss Edward Doubleday at the British Museum. What now the good find of another specimen for him to have, Ken thought.

By noon en route back to Green Mountain Falls the two stopped for lunch beneath the Whispering Tree, then rest a bit with Sally's head upon his shoulder and an arm across him. That, perhaps, was to be the last time for such closeness before Ken would leave on the morrow to return to England.

"Do you still need to go back to England?" Sally asked.

"You knew from the start that my trip here was to be a short one in order to get Apollo specimens for the museum back quickly before their bodies dry too much, but even then they will likely be in need of softening for dissections of inner parts."

"But how can you do that?"

"Not me, but Mr. Doubleday. He's the one who will make the dissections and what he will do is rather simple. He will put about two inches of sand into the bottom of a container sort of like a wide-mouthed cookie jar and wet the sand thoroughly. On top of that he will put a double layer of paper and on top of that the butterflies needed to soften. The jar will be closed for twenty-four hours and kept in a dry cool place such as down in a cellar to help retard mold and then checked to see if softened enough already. If not, and after another day stored they should be soft enough to spread their wings for displays in glass cases or for dissections. Voila! That's all there is to it. But hey! It's time for another wade in the creek.

When back in the valley Sally went to her hotel room to bathe and to freshen up, and to return with prairie chicken dinners courtesy of the hotel and in Sally's remembrance of their first meal together in the Antlers. "Surprise!" She said.

"Ken...if you must go back tomorrow how will you go?"

"By the Midland to Colorado Springs and Denver, then by the Union Pacific to New York. From there I'm scheduled to sail on the Cunard Line *Etruria* which is the newest and fastest liner in service between New York and Liverpool taking only six days. From there I'll take the London and Southwestern Railway directly home. It's been long planned to get the Apollos back to London the quickest way."

"Isn't mailing them back just as quick?"

"Not nearly or as safe. Packages get tossed around in mail rooms and when going overseas on the proverbial slow boats to China they get stored in damp areas where mildew can be problems. I'm instructed to hand carry them the entire way back to England to insure they arrive in good condition."

"When you get there will you write to me about your trip back, your museum work and everything about the Apollos?"

"Yes...of course...a long letter."

"I'll write to you about my hotel job and all."

"For tonight however," Ken suggested, "we should retire early since my train for Colorado Springs leaves at nine in the morning. We can yet play a few card games before bedtime and have breakfast together. I'll take the pallet again and you the bed."

"More card games would be fun, and thanks for the bed offer, but if I go back now to the hotel for the night I can bring breakfast in the morning that will save us some time."

"There is no need for that when pancakes and coffee are quick to prepare and we'll still have time tonight for a card game or two before an early bedtime. It's just a suggestion, though, that maybe...well...maybe we...oh never mind. It's just a thought."

"What? Tell me anyway!"

"It's just that...well...maybe for this last night we can skip the card games and forget the pallet."

• • • •

After a breakfast with Sally making the pancakes and Ken the coffee little time remained to get to the Midland depot by which time steam whistles of the train coming down from Woodland Park could already be heard from afar. Even less time now remained for expressions of last minute difficult-to-profess goodbyes and a long embrace with final last words.

"Ken...last night...did you mean what you said, that you will never forget me."

"Our palling around together this month was full of fun times that can never be forgotten. How could they? I will always remember them, and especially you."

"Me too, and you, but will we ever see one another again...ever?"

Afterword

[Fifteen years later, Denver]
"Do you still remember when we first met?"
Kenneth Stanley.
"Yes. It was the day you first saw me and said 'hello.'"
Sally Ruth.
"What do you remember most of us?" He asked.
"Our hikes up along the Crystal Creek water falls,
the lake and gazebo, the Midland trains, being square
dance partners, and when riding horses and collecting
butterflies together...and you of course for everything."
"Me too, and especially you.
Someday I'll write a story about it all."

In Memoriam

References

Cafky, Morris.
1965. *Colorado Midland*. World Press, Denver. 467pp.

Colorado Midland Railway. Wikipedia. 2pp.

Discovering Ute Pass Volume 1: Tales of Lower Ute Pass.
2016. Ute Pass Historical Society & Pikes Peak Museum, Woodland Park, Colorado. 200pp.

Field Guide to the Butterflies and Other Insects of Britain.
1984. Readers Digest Association Limited. London New York. 352pp.

Holland, W.J.
1898. *The Butterfly Book*. Doubleday & Company Inc. Garden City New York. 424pp and 78 Plates.

Matter, Stephen F. *et. al.*
2012. Young Love? Mating of *Parnassius smintheus* Doubleday (Papilionidae). Journal of the Lepidopterist's Society.

Parnassius smintheus.
Editing Parnassius smintheus. Wikipedia 5pp.

Pyle, Robert Michael.
1981. *Field Guide to North American Butterflies.* National Audubon Society. 927pp.

Roslin, Thomas *et. al.*
2008. Caterpillars on the run...spatial patterns in host plant damage. Ecography. 13pp.

Strecker, Herman.
1878. *Butterflies and Moths of North America*. Press of B.F. Owen. 283pp.

Ute Pass History.
Ute Pass Historical Society. Internet 5pp

About the Author and Story

James Kaye is a retired research biologist from the National Park Service working first in Carlsbad Caverns, then Padre Island, Joshua Tree, Death Valley, Channel Islands and lastly Hawaii Volcanoes National Park, during which Kaye wrote thirty papers in science journals on plant and animal subjects.

Other interests were (are) in the art of British artist John William Waterhouse with three papers on his life and works in art journals; two being in The British Art Journal.

Kaye also wrote five articles on the 1800s pioneer era of Texas, his home State, appearing in history journals and four novels based on Texas history; one being *A British Butterfly Collector on the Texas Frontier.*

When a teenager, Kaye collected butterflies in Texas and of the obstacles encountered as written in the Dedication to all collectors of them. In 1948 on a summer vacation trip in Green Mountain Falls and when Midland trains were still running through the town, and when on hikes up along the Crystal Creek waterfalls, Kaye collected specimens of the so-called Rocky Mountain Apollos commonly known as The Snow Butterfly of the Mountains (**Fig. 33**). His interest in them and in the history of Green Mountain Falls as  well as that of Ute Pass inspired much of the storylines in *The Falls of Green Mountain* Novella, sometimes known as a "long short story."